*C*aring
FOR YOURSELF
WHILE *C*aring FOR
YOUR AGING PARENTS

Also by Claire Berman

A HOLE IN MY HEART:
    ADULT CHILDREN OF DIVORCE SPEAK OUT

MAKING IT AS A STEPPARENT

"WHAT AM I DOING IN A STEPFAMILY?"

WE TAKE THIS CHILD:
    A CANDID LOOK AT MODERN ADOPTION

Claire Berman

Caring

FOR YOURSELF

WHILE *Caring* FOR

YOUR AGING PARENTS

☙ ❧

How to Help,
How to Survive

Henry Holt and Company
New York

Henry Holt and Company, Inc.
Publishers since 1866
115 West 18th Street
New York, New York 10011

Henry Holt® is a registered
trademark of Henry Holt and Company, Inc.

LIBRARY OF CONGRESS CATALOGING-IN-PUBLICATION DATA
Berman, Claire.
Caring for yourself while caring for your aging parents: how to help,
how to survive/Claire Berman.—1st ed.
p. cm.
Includes bibliographical references and index.
1. Aging parents—Care—United States.   2. Caregivers—United States—
Psychology.   3. Parent and adult child—United States. I. Title.
HV1461.b48   1996   95-32613
362.6—dc20   CIP

ISBN 0-8050-3734-9

Henry Holt books are available for special promotions
and premiums. For details contact:
Director, Special Markets.

First Edition—1996

Designed by Kathryn Parise

Printed in the United States of America
All first editions are printed on acid-free paper.∞

10   9   8   7   6   5   4   3   2

To Noel

CONTENTS

ACKNOWLEDGMENTS

This book was written with the assistance and encouragement of many people. Foremost among them are the women
and men—children of ailing and aged parents—who wel-
comed me into their lives and shared with me (and my readers) their stories of caregiving, both practical and emotional.
To encourage candor, I promised anonymity, and so I cannot
name them here. But I'd like the caregivers to know how
very grateful I am, and I hope they will feel that I have used
their information well.

Many of these same people reached out to introduce me
to others among their acquaintances who were also striving
to meet the challenges of parent care. To them, a double
thank-you. Appreciation is also extended to Lynne Dumas,
Anne Finger, Mark Fuerst, Elaine Kramer, Ellen Rodman, and
Evelyn Umlas, who pointed me in helpful directions.

Nick Newcombe, my mom's first social worker, was there
for me from the start. When I first thought about doing this
book, he encouraged me. And when I looked out at the wide
caregiving landscape I would have to cover and found it
daunting, Nick helped me to place things in perspective. In
the process, Nick has become a cherished friend.

Anna (Honey) Zimmer was most generous in offering
time and information at various points during the research
and writing of this book. A consummate professional, she
too helped me focus on the issues.

Karen J. Alexander, senior transit planner at Urbitran Associates, shared information on transportation services for the disabled and elderly, then continued to alert me to people, programs, and publications that would be of further use. Linda Greenman, former director of the Caregiver's Center at Dorot, opened her program and the organization's library to me. To Caroline Messner of Cancer Care go thanks for providing direction.

Judith Brickman, with the New York City Department for the Aging, discovered during our meeting that we had known one another as teenagers. An old friend, she became a current mentor, as did her able colleague Olevia Smith. Rea Kahn of the Alzheimer's Association is someone to whom I frequently turn for knowledge and support, and who constantly comes through for me and others.

I am thankful to Rose Dobrof, who wears so many professional hats (and with such style!), for sharing her knowledge and insights, and for introducing me to Robert Butler, whose intelligence enriches me and whose vision inspires me. Many other scholars, researchers, and practitioners were generous with their time and information. Their contributions are cited throughout this work.

I am grateful to my agent, Jim Levine, for his encouragement and support, and to Arielle Eckstut and Melissa Rowland of his office for their unfailing good humor at the other end of the line. Special thanks to Dan Greenberg for his energy. Cynthia Vartan, my editor, was enthusiastic about this book from the moment she received the proposal, and thereafter knew when (and when not) to step in. I appreciate that.

The contributions of Joan and Richard Lees, Sybil Sigman, and Sam and Elaine Gallant are too many to be enumerated. "Thank you" is all I can say, yet I know it is not enough.

My family has ever been a strong source of personal support for me, managing to bridge the miles that often separate us in ways that constantly assure me of their interest and encouragement. To my children—Orin, Mitch and Ingrid, Eric and Liz—go my thanks and my love, with enough, always, in reserve for Noel Berman, my best friend.

Finally, I want to acknowledge two incredible women, Rebecca Gallant and Rose Hazel Berman, for a lifetime of caring.

Caring
FOR YOURSELF
WHILE Caring FOR
YOUR AGING PARENTS

INTRODUCTION

You have to take care of yourself. If you don't take care of yourself, you won't be able to take care of another person.
—Dorothy Calvani, former staff nurse in the Geriatric Clinic of New York's Mt. Sinai Hospital, comforting the adult child of an Alzheimer's patient

I am that adult child.

At the time of this writing, I am fifty-eight years old. My mother, Rebecca, age ninety, has been widowed for close to three decades, almost from the age that I am now. She has been suffering from dementia for the last half dozen of those years. It's Alzheimer's disease, according to the many doctors that Mom and I have visited during this time. Of course, they add, only an autopsy can absolutely confirm the diagnosis, which has become irrelevant. More to the point is this overwhelming reality: my mother's in a bad way, and she's slowly getting worse.

My mother-in-law, Hazel, now ninety-eight, suffers from a host of problems resulting from the deterioration of the machine that is her body. Simply, and sadly, the parts are wearing out. You could open a pharmacy with the medication and pills that this frail woman must take each day just to make it to the next morning. "Old age is hell," she tells me one day when we speak on the phone. She begins to cry.

Both women were once capable, outgoing, and highly independent.

Now each is widowed, ill, painfully lonely, and very much in need of attention and care. And I? I feel consumed by their situation.

But most of all, I feel *guilty*.

GUILTY because whatever I do for "the mothers" (as I've come to refer to them in conversations with my own grown sons), I know it is not enough.

GUILTY because I permit both my sister and sister-in-law ("the saints") to do too much.

GUILTY because of my periodic outrage at a much-loved brother when I have felt he wasn't doing enough.

GUILTY because I'm healthy and able to go out to the movies and enjoy dinner with friends when my mother sits alone, at night, in her home.

GUILTY because I've come to view visits to my mother and mother-in-law as an obligation. (At the same time, I worry that my sons will feel similarly one day about visiting me.)

I also find myself feeling *angry*.

I FEEL ANGER when my mother, who was always neat and well-groomed, insists on wearing the same soiled red woolen jacket day in and day out.

I FEEL ANGER when I find myself pressed to respond, once again, to a question that Mom has asked six times within a period of three minutes. (First I feel impatience, then annoyance, then a rising anger. I feel badgered.)

I FEEL ANGER when I'm forced to shout because my mother refuses to wear the hearing aid we had obtained after she and I sat through interminable visits at hearing clinics, after we had seen a private doctor, after we had spent a lot of time and a ridiculous amount of money to have the proper aids made. "Talk louder," my mother says to me, to her doctors, to the speaker at the senior center that she sometimes attends. I find my temperature rising when each doctor who newly examines my mother turns to me and advises, "Your mother really needs a hearing aid." I feel exasperated.

Then I feel guilty about reacting with anger and resentment.

I FEEL FRUSTRATED when, after successfully arranging for a housekeeper to provide Mom with much-needed assistance two mornings a week, my mother sends the woman away, insisting that she does not need any help. (I feel terribly sad, now, because Mom has moved on to needing, and accepting, the services of a home-care attendant seven days a week.)

I FEEL FRUSTRATED when, each time the issue is raised, my mother flatly refuses to move out of her apartment when my sister has lovingly offered Mom a place in her own home. I feel frustrated even though I know that, in rejecting help, my mother is clutching fiercely to what remains of her independence, her personhood. I also feel that help must come from another quarter. My sister is not well enough to care for our mother on a full-time basis. And I am not prepared to make the commitment.

Which explains, in large part, why I also feel *unworthy*. "Thank you, thank you," my mother tells me whenever I do the littlest thing, like calling each day to check on her welfare. "How are you?" I ask when she answers the phone.

"Now that *you* called, I'm much better," she responds. "You made my day."

I handle the doctors' visits for Mom because, it's generally acknowledged in the family, I am good at research, at organization. In fact, I FEEL DISHEARTENED by my inability to organize my mother's life, to know what it is that *should* be done, and then to help by implementing the necessary changes, to make things right for her.

More and more, of late, I have found myself feeling *helpless*. In the past several months, for example, my mother has taken to asking in our every conversation, morning or evening, on the phone or in person, "So what is there for me to do with the day?" She wants a plan. She wants direction for her life. And all I can do is answer: Go to the senior center; read the newspaper; and (if it isn't too windy or cold out, if I'm not concerned that she will fall) go for a walk.

I FEEL POWERLESS because I cannot shape her life. And because I do not know, in this situation, what there is for *each* of us to do.

At times, I find myself wondering not so much whether my mother will make it through a particular day, but whether *I* will. I FEEL OVERWHELMED.

A recent experience serves as an example. I'd arrived at my mother's home to drive her to the geriatric clinic. Despite having phoned Mom the previous evening and twice that morning to alert her to the fact that I'd be coming by, when I let myself into her apartment she expressed surprise at seeing me. She then took a long time getting ready, changing one sweater for another, topping it off with the red woolen jacket, while I grew impatient. An hour's drive lay before us.

Heading uptown on the FDR Drive, a twisty, narrow highway bordering Manhattan's East River, I glanced in the rearview mirror to locate the motorcycle I'd been hearing. There was no motorcycle in sight. The rumbling sounds were coming from *my* car. Was it the exhaust? The engine? My concern grew.

All the while, Mom kept up a barrage of questions: *Have you heard from your children lately? Where are they living? What are they doing? How is your mother-in-law? Do you think it will rain tomorrow? It looks like it will rain tomorrow. Did you speak to your mother-in-law lately?* As I answered each question, my mind centered on the image of two stranded women, one in a red woolen jacket, standing by the side of the highway, thumbs extended, as hundreds of cars whizzed by. When at long last we made it to a parking lot near the hospital, the car was in far better condition than I was.

Nurse Dorothy Calvani greeted Mom warmly. "Hello, Rebecca, you're looking great," she said. She then turned to me. "Your mother looks fine," she said, the dimples in her cheeks deepening with the warmth of her smile.

"Yes, she does," I replied through gritted teeth. "*I'm* the one who's about to jump out a window."

Dorothy's expression turned serious. "Let's talk," she said quietly, taking a seat beside me in the busy waiting room where white-haired men and women and their caregivers, seated in rows of orange plastic chairs, gazed listlessly at the walls adorned by posters proclaiming the importance of good nutrition and exercise.

Talk we did. I told the nurse about my emotional state. She listened. She didn't criticize. She spoke to me about the possibility of my joining a support group for caregivers. In fact, just talking with Dorothy helped me feel calmer, better. After leaving the clinic, I drove my mother home. The car rumbled even louder on the return trip. Yes, the problem was still there. Only now I felt as if I'd be able to handle it.

That is the kind of support that I hope you, the reader, will find in this book. I hope you will feel listened to, enlightened, and supported. I hope it will help you to cope.

Knowledge Is Power

If you are reading this book, chances are that at the very least you're concerned about your parent's physical or mental condition and wonder if, and how, you should step in. More likely, you're already involved, either providing direct care or directing the provision of care by others. Each time you think you've managed a problem, another one crops up.

When parents reach the point where adult children find it necessary to intervene in their behalf, those same children quickly discover a whole world of knowledge that they must plug into. These concrete issues include such matters as: learning about the specific disability; finding the right doctor; identifying appropriate social services; locating capable caretakers; helping parents manage their finances; dealing with bureaucracies; filling out forms; investigating adult day care; and, if necessary, researching residential facilities.

Many books and organizations deal with these issues, and I have found myself turning to them for information as needed. (A suggested reading list appears in Appendix D, page 241.) You will find a great deal of practical information in this book, as well. Because the focus throughout is to help you, the caregiver, care for yourself, it is important to provide as much direction as possible.

"Knowledge is power," says Dr. Lori Bright-Long, director of Geriatric Psychiatry at New York's Pilgrim State Hospital. She tells caregivers, "If you don't have any strength or energy or you don't know any way that you can face the problems, you will become much more overwhelmed than if you say to yourself, 'Yes, I've got something I can do, I've got some power in this situation.'" **Information is one of the most important coping mechanisms you can have.**

Concrete vs. Emotional Issues

Studies have shown, however, that adult children, as a group, are far less distressed by the practical, financial, and physical aspects of caregiving than they are by the emotional aspects. Take the feeling of guilt, for example. It may be the most pervasive of all among the population of caregivers—even the most devoted of whom find reason, at times, to ask themselves: *Did I do enough?* All too often, they answer in the negative.

My friend Ellen, fifty-four, unquestionably qualifies for inclusion in the "most devoted" category. After her eighty-four-year-old mother, Sophie, was operated on for removal of a malignant uterine tumor, with chemotherapy to follow, Ellen took a leave of absence from teaching in order to move in with the older woman and care for her. Ellen shopped, cooked, and played endless rounds of rummy 500 with her mother.

One day, as Sophie was walking out of the bathroom, she stumbled, fracturing her right arm, which she'd thrust forward to break her fall. *I should have been there*, Ellen repeatedly rebuked herself, even though she'd been standing in the kitchen, only a few yards away, when the accident occurred. Ellen felt as culpable, perhaps even more so, as the son or daughter who lives at a distance from an aging parent and has to find out in a phone call from the parent's neighbor that Mom or Dad has fallen and been taken to the hospital.

Those who care for aging parents would do well to accept that there will always be some amount of guilt. The point is, guilt happens. Anger happens. Frustration happens. Depression happens. Weariness certainly happens. The trick is to make much of the good moments, also, when *they* happen, for in caregiving there can also be moments of closeness, moments of sharing, fleeting moments of exchange or understanding, moments in which love also happens.

Who Is a Caregiver?

Anna H. Zimmer, director of the Institute on Mutual Aid/Self Help of The Brookdale Center on Aging at New York's Hunter College, defines *caregiver* as "someone who is involved in helping someone else manage to carry out the tasks of living." In a normal situation, for example, the parent is caregiver to the young child, who needs help with multiple tasks in learning to negotiate his or her way in the world. The turnaround, which we consider here, centers on the parent who has grown older, frailer, and more dependent, and on the shift that takes place in family relationships when you find yourself caring for the mother or father who once cared for you.

Adult sons and daughters fitting the caregiver description include: the daughter who lives halfway across the country, hires a geriatric care manager, and places a weekly phone call to her ailing father; the son who goes in once a month to balance his mother's checkbook; the daughter who does all the marketing or who arranges for, and oversees, the hired attendant; the daughter-in-law who chauffeurs her father-in-law to his adult day-care program; the daughter who pays regular visits to the nursing home where her mother now resides; and the adult child who shares a home with the frail elderly parent, providing round-the-clock assistance so demanding and debilitating that it is often referred to as "the thirty-six-hour day."

Amy Horowitz, D.S.W., director of the Lighthouse Research Institute, conceptualizes caregiving behavior as falling into four broad categories: emotional support; direct service provision; mediation with formal organizations and providers; and financial assistance. Sharing a household, which she lists as a special form of caregiving, might encompass all of the above.

Research has consistently shown that, in any family, *one* member occupies the role of primary caregiver—the relative to whom the older person turns for assistance when needed and who actually provides the most help. More often than not, that role is filled by the less-impaired spouse (when present) until the burden becomes overwhelming. Then, it is taken over by the adult sons and daughters.

Geriatric care manager Nick Newcombe observes, "Sometimes just one sibling is doing the actual toileting, changing, bathing, financial management, all of that, and the other sibling is clear across the country, trying to be supportive or, in some cases, seeming to remain uninvolved. Still, it can be very hard for the passive caregiver to deal with his own emotions. The active caregiver can at least work out the relationship with the parent on a daily basis."

Active or passive, we are fast becoming a nation of care-givers. And our numbers are legion.

We live at a time when there are so many older people, the term "aged" itself has had to be subdivided into "young old," "middle old," and "old old." Many of us, as we grow older, are fortunate enough to have our parents with us for a very long time. The pleasure of having parents around to continue to share in our lives is evident, especially when the elder parent remains alert, able, and active, as is so often the case.

One of my acquaintances recently traveled to Europe with her mother, a woman in her nineties. Another friend continues to enjoy a round of golf with his father, who is ninety-two and still goes in to work every day. And the father of yet another acquaintance just celebrated his eighty-fifth birthday by remarrying and heading off on a honeymoon cruise with his seventy-nine-year-old bride. Clearly, many older people lead productive, active lives. May we all be thus blessed.

But the fact is that the preponderance of stories about parents that I hear from my contemporaries, and from people who straddle both sides of my decade, has to do less with accompanying Mother to Paris than with arranging for Mom to see yet another doctor, to take yet another medication, to make it through yet another day. The challenge of longevity is that it is often accompanied by serious ailments, such as memory disorders, malignancies, and chronic diseases. Many of us find that our older parents need our help not just occasionally but on a continuing basis.

A Nation of Caregivers

Although the reality of the aging of America is well known, a look at some actual statistics serves to present a clearer picture of the magnitude of the challenge we are facing. In 1994, there were about 33 million Americans over the age of 65. According to the U.S. Census Bureau, that number is expected to more than double, to about 75 million people over the next 40 years. The population of people 85 and older, now more than 3 million, will more than triple, to over 11 million. Some 54,000 of our citizens have celebrated the one-hundredth anniversary of their birth. By the year 2030 (again, according to the Census Bureau), that number is projected to increase to 477,000; ten years later to 660,000. "Centenarians have become the fastest-growing segment of the population among the industrialized countries," according to Leonard W. Poon, director of the gerontology center at the University of Georgia. All of this has led *The Economist* magazine to declare, "A new human age, the super-old, is fast becoming reality."

People are not just living longer; they are living longer with disability. Failing hearing and eyesight are but two of the issues that plague the old and require them to seek assistance. Failing memory, especially after the age of eighty-five, is particularly devastating. Medical advances are keeping alive people who in another time would have died quickly of cancer, stroke, or heart attack. Nowadays, we lose our parents bit by bit.

What we're looking at is a society in which the old increasingly will be seeing to the needs of the very old *and* the super-old. (Over half of caregivers are past the age of sixty-five, according to a 1989 report by the Older Women's League.) That's a very different picture than the popular image of caregivers, by and large, as members of "the sandwich generation"—men and women who are weighed down by the needs of children on the one hand and of parents on the other. Reality requires a broader frame, one able to accommodate a larger group of people, including: the wife who is torn between spending time with a retired spouse and time with a frail, dependent parent; the working person who juggles job demands with filial obligations (a Canadian study predicts that by the year 2000, 77 percent of employees will have some type of responsibility for elderly relatives); childless spouses; single men and women; "children" facing the assaults of the process of their own aging. We caregivers are members of a very large company.

This book introduces women and men who, like you, are struggling with the challenges of parent care. Their stories and their insights, born of experience, make up much of the material. Although I have changed the names and clearly identifying descriptions of the people I interviewed, I have retained their wisdom and their own words throughout.

The questions I asked of them had to do with their own work and family situation, their parents' situation, the caregiving role, its effect on home and work obligations, support and stress in the sibling situation, present and past history of the parent/child relationship, feelings of loss and mourning, financial matters, and more, so much more. And always, in every interview, I sought to find out: *What program or person has been most beneficial? Who and what has helped you to cope?*

Not surprisingly, the answers varied widely. The daughter or daughter-in-law whose own children are in school and who drops in daily on Mom is faced with different pressures than the single woman who lives several states distant from her mother and cannot take time off from work to make frequent visits. The son or son-in-law assisting a housebound parent faces different concerns than the adult child whose parent *is* able to get out of the house but may not remember the way back home. The type of disability, financial circumstances, geography, cooperation among siblings . . . these are just some of the many factors that make each caregiving challenge, and response, unique.

Within this variety, however, one is startled by how often the same experiences are repeated, the same feelings are described. In hearing others' stories, in listening to the men and women I met in support groups and to those who took the time to share their experiences with me, time and again I found myself thinking, *This is how I feel, too; this is what I am going through*. The recognition that one is not alone, the knowledge that certain deeply felt responses to events and circumstances are shared, that they are normal, can be therapeutic. I return to these voices time and again, when I am in need, and hope that you will, too.

I have spotted the accounts throughout the narrative. Not surprisingly, the story lines frequently intersect, falling under more than one category. For example, a person who's a supercaregiver (see chapter 1) may also carry the burdens of an only child (chapter 4); a long-distance caregiver (chapter 5) may also be experiencing some tension in dealing with his siblings (chapter 3). I have placed the various case histories where it seems to me that they best fit, knowing that there will be a certain overlap. As you use this book, please do not pass up the sections that seem not to relate to you. They may contain suggestions, and solutions, that will ease your way during this time.

Daughters are more strongly represented among the caregivers you will meet here. This is true for society as a whole, where three quarters of informal caregivers are female. Researchers explain this difference by citing women's traditional role as nurturers; their stronger emotional ties to the family of origin; and their availability to provide care. (This is becoming less the case as more women enter the workforce.)

Men who take on the role of primary caregiver tend to be those who are only children, or who have been raised in an all-male household, or who live geographically closest to the parent. Studies show, however, that when a family has only sons, the daughter-in-law is much more likely to take responsibility for reliant elders. Other family members, if involved at all, play secondary roles.

You'll also find mothers outnumbering fathers among the frail elderly people whom you meet in these pages. This, too, is the general case. It rests on several factors, among them: women tend to live longer; they marry men older than themselves, and care for them when they become ill. Women are also less likely than men to remarry following the death of a partner, with the result that their care is more apt to fall to adult children or other relatives.

Finding Peace with Yourself

The time spent in caring for an aged mother or father, the intimacy imposed by the arrangement, forces many of us to confront feelings that have lain dormant for years, perhaps decades. "Sometimes you love someone and do not tell them," says a daughter whose mother was disabled by a series of strokes. "Caring for my mother allows me to show her how much she matters. It is my chance to give something back."

Others whose relationship with a parent was not quite as close use this time to gain a better understanding of, and improved relationship with, a parent. I believe that this is one result of the time I am now spending with my mother. In caring for her needs, I have come to care more about her as a human being, and as my mother. In some perverse fashion, I am glad to have been given this chance.

And then there are adult children, like Wilma, who rail against the situation they now find themselves in. At age fifty-two, Wilma drops in daily on her eighty-four-year-old mother, who suffers from Parkinson's disease. (A health-care aide stays with the older woman at night.) "Whenever I'm with my mother, a self-centered woman who's always been more interested in herself than in me, I find my throat constricting and I have trouble breathing," Wilma says, "and yet there I am, dancing attendance upon her as always. You'd think that at this stage of my life she would no longer have this hold on me." Wilma's anger is debilitating and must be addressed. Joining a support group and seeking professional counseling are two actions that Wilma should consider in order to survive her mother's illness.

Reconciliation between parent and child is not always feasible. Resolution is another matter. This book speaks to the importance of resolving the relationship with a parent. Resolution enables the adult child to do a responsible job, to delegate certain tasks, and to move forward toward his or her own future with the increased self-respect that comes from knowing that *you did the best you could.* That is all we can ask of ourselves.

Caring for an aging parent is a balancing act. The primary intent of this book is to help you, the caregiver, come away with the confidence and tools that make it possible to achieve a workable, livable balance between meeting your needs and addressing the needs of your parent. There's just no getting around it: **If we are to successfully manage the care of our parents, we have to learn, first of all, to care for ourselves.**

CHAPTER 1

SUPERCAREGIVERS:
STRUGGLES AND SUCCESSES

As other children grow up with fairy tales, I spent my early years listening to family stories about Bubbe Rachel, my father's mother, who made her home with my parents from the day they were wed until the day that she died, some fifteen years later, in my first year of life. As recalled for me by my parents and older siblings, my bubbe was a wonderful woman: straight of stature, sage, caring, and supportive. It was Bubbe Rachel who taught Mom how to run a house and manage three children. My mother's face lights up today at the mention of her name. When my grandmother began to fail, this same family she had cared for so lovingly was there to return the favor.

My husband tells me about his maternal grandfather, Grandpa Nathan, a widower who made his home with three unmarried daughters. The women prepared his meals, gave him his medication, saw to it that he had his newspaper at the ready, and otherwise made it possible for the older man to spend his afternoons sitting outside, talking with his cronies. In the once-upon-a-time that is our heritage, such dedicated caregiving was unremarkable.

It is not uncommon today, as well, but the pressures of modern life seem to be different and the provision of care more complicated than in times past. As has been noted, women (the traditional caregivers) have joined the labor force in great numbers. Children grow up, move away, and live at a distance from their parents. Further, our parents live longer with debilitating illnesses. The wonder is that so many adult children continue to make such extraordinary commitments to their parents' care, often at the expense of self-care.

This chapter introduces you to the supercaregivers, to their struggles, and to the ways that some have found to lighten the burden.

Meet Joel and Sharon Stayman

"Had we realized then what we know now, we probably would have done things differently. We would have found some other way to care for my father-in-law than to have him come live with us."

The speaker, Sharon Stayman, is a comely woman in her mid-fifties. She sits next to her husband, Joel, who looks younger than his fifty-seven years, in the sunlit family room of their split-level house outside Philadelphia. The home has the cared-for, orderly appearance often found in households where the children have grown up and moved out.

On the mantel over the fireplace are framed photographs of the Stayman family: a bridal portrait of their daughter, Dena, and her husband, Brian, taken five years earlier; son David at his college graduation two years ago; their two-year-old granddaughter, Michelle, smiling from the confines of a backyard swing; sepia-tinted portraits of Sharon's late mother and father. To the right, in a silver frame, is a picture of Ben, Joel's father. Ben moved in with this family when he was seventy-five and was cared for by them until his final illness ten years later.

The arrangement was arrived at by agreement, not design. A victim of severe vision loss, which affects almost 3.5 million Americans aged 65 and older, Ben suffered from age-related macular degeneration; legally blind, he had only peripheral vision left. Over the years, as his sight diminished, he had come to rely more and more on his wife, Helen, and when she died, he grew panicky at the prospect of having to manage on his own. "I take cheese out of the refrigerator and don't know if it's spoiled or not," he told his son Joel. Nor could his sense of smell alert him, since it was not much stronger than his eyesight.

For more than a year after becoming a widower, Ben roomed with another man, but would spend every Thursday, Friday, and Saturday with Joel's family. (Sharon cooked meals to last him the rest of the week.) Then, following a gallbladder operation, he went from the hospital to their home to recuperate; while there, he asked to remain permanently. "The way my father looked at it, family has got to take care of family," says Joel.

"So that's just how it had to be," adds Sharon. "We had no choice." And so Ben and his children became part of a growing statistic: one out of seven people over the age of sixty-five lives with a son or daughter; for those eighty-five and older, that number is much higher; for women it is higher still. One out of every four women over the age of eighty-five lives with an adult child.

Should a Parent Move in with You? Some Considerations . . .

The decision to have elderly parents move in with adult children must be made cautiously and after a lot of planning, say the experts. Several factors should be considered, chief among them the often complicated preexisting relationship. If, based on past experiences, there is ill will between parent and child or if there's a problem with communication, living together is likely to create added stress. A different arrangement should be considered for *everyone's* sake.

Another factor in considering whether to bring a parent to live with the adult child has to do with how long the parent has resided in his or her home or neighborhood, and the support system that exists where they are. Loneliness is a big problem for the elderly, who frequently do better where they can continue to see old friends and neighbors. Also important to their well-being are familiar places: the house of worship where they've traditionally gone to seek comfort; the local bank; the tailor or shoe repair shop that they've patronized for years. Doctors Amy Horowitz and Barbara Silverstone have written about people "aging in place," meaning that they grow old in the old neighborhood. For many elders, the gerontologists point out, familiar surroundings often become one's security.

The Staymans gave little thought to such matters and believe now that they all would have fared better if there had first been some discussion, some deliberation, about the advisability of the move. "In hindsight," says Sharon, "I think we should have arranged to bring in someone who could help care for my father-in-law in his own apartment. Relocating to our home separated Pop from all his friends and isolated him, and that was bad for him."

Privacy became an immediate issue for the family. For one thing, the home they then lived in—a compact ranch of the kind that real estate agents generally refer to as a "starter" house—was a snug-enough fit for two parents and two growing children. (Dena was nine and David six and a half when their grandfather came to stay.) It could not accommodate another adult, especially one who was in constant danger of tripping over the children's playthings, and who needed quiet and care. "We considered building out," Joel says, "but decided instead to move to this split-level home because it had a den that we could convert to a bedroom and bathroom for my father. We needed our own space and closed doors, and so did he. Pop paid for the renovation."

Even with the new arrangement, privacy became a remembered luxury for the caregivers. Their daily life now had an audience. Their free time was circumscribed. They took to having friends in because it was just too hard to arrange an evening out. When people visited, however, Ben invariably would join the gathering, nodding off as the evening wore on. Their friends would leave early. In desperation, the young couple set aside Saturday night as a time apart. No matter what, they decided, they would go out and do something together. "Saturday nights are what saved our sanity," says Sharon.

It was not, however, salvation without cost, for on Saturday nights the kids would be home with their grandfather, whose child-raising philosophy differed sharply from their parents'. Joel says, "We'd come home to find my father sitting up in his pajamas, waiting to tell on the children: 'Dena watched too much television' . . . 'David didn't want to go to sleep. He's still up.' Pop wouldn't yell at David. He would just sit there. Our son kept asking us, 'Why doesn't Grandpa go to sleep?' He felt guilty that his grandfather was staying up because of him. It became a stressful situation."

During the week, Joel, an accountant, was hardly ever at home. To make ends meet, he juggled several jobs and would often see clients in the evening. The major responsibility for Ben's care and social life fell to Sharon, a former editor who now found herself busier than ever as a homemaker and full-time caregiver.

"I'm the one who would take Pop for a haircut, I would take him to the doctor, I'd take him for everything," she says. "I was his maid, his chauffeur, his company keeper. I felt I had no life of my own, and I was unable to go out and find one. At times, I would complain to Joel about being tied down, being unable to go back to work, which would have been good for my sanity and our finances.

"Then, when I'd find myself feeling most resentful, I would look at this gentle man and feel guilty because, with it all, there were some very special times, some very warm moments between us. These were the afternoons when the kids were in school and Pop and I would sit together and talk. I'd ask him about his childhood, and he would tell me wonderful stories. We had a rapport, he and I. You can't spend all that time with someone without growing very close. And we did."

When Siblings Don't Share

"Sharon was the good person, and I became the bad one, because I wasn't around very much," Joel says. "But best of all in Pop's estimation was my brother, Harry, because he placed a phone call once a week." Mention of Joel's brother serves as a signal for Sharon to get up and go into the kitchen. It's as if she still needs to place some distance between herself and the subject.

"Harry is a history professor who lives with his wife and three sons in Durham, North Carolina," Joel explains. "Five years older than I am, he was always a school ahead of me. When I was in high school, he was in college. When I was in college, he was in graduate school. I got the feeling that he always felt a bit superior to me . . . which I could live with, except that he and I had a mother and father in common, and the father happened to require a great deal of care. Harry would call once a week, and Pop would come away from the phone glowing."

The absence of brotherly support brought additional strain into the Stayman home, with Sharon being the principal protester. "I grew up as an only child," she says, returning with a fresh pot of coffee. "I always thought it would be wonderful to have a sister or brother, someone who could be there to support you, who would be your closest friend. But here was Joel with all the responsibility, and his older brother did practically nothing and *offered* to do nothing. That hurt."

There came a time when Joel didn't wait for an offer. "The whole family needed some respite if we were going to keep our sanity," he says. "So I phoned my brother and I told him, 'It's our anniversary and we're going away. I'm putting Pop on a plane and you have to be there to meet it.' I initiated the visit, I was firm, and it became a precedent. From then on, Pop always stayed with Harry for two weeks in December and again for two weeks in the summer when we would take a trip with the children. That was really important."

Geriatric psychiatrist Lori Bright-Long confirms the importance to caregivers of coming out and asking for the help that is needed. She explains, "Often people never even ask for help. Instead, we retreat into magical thinking when it has to do with family relationships. We think, *You ought to have known that I needed help with Mom,* and then feel resentful when the help that we wish for isn't forthcoming. If we *do* ask for help, we're vague about what we need. People say, 'I need help,' when they ought to say, 'Hey, I need you to watch Mom on a Saturday while I go out and do something' or 'I need you to chip in some bucks each month because I know you can't come in from Poughkeepsie to help out, and I have to hire someone.'

"The sibling who lives farther away, or the one who's not as emotionally involved, really doesn't know what kind of help you need," she continues. "The caregiver has to ask for help and be specific. If you state concrete needs, often people will come through." (For a further discussion of sibling relationships, see chapter 3.)

Joel also busied himself with finding aids that would help his father live a fuller life. Tape recorders, talking books, anything that would let some light into the older man's narrowing world was researched and obtained. Learning about an illness, learning what's out there that can enrich the patient's life, provides the parent with help and the caregiver with satisfaction.

But more was needed to enrich the quality of Ben's life. Sharon spent days, weeks, months driving her father-in-law the length and width of the Philadelphia suburbs, looking for a golden-age club, a senior center, some place where Ben could find age-appropriate companionship. . . . "And none of them clicked," she says. "Pop always found fault, whether it was the basket weaving, the card playing, the fact that he couldn't see, whatever. 'Not for me,' he would say, and that would be the end of it.

The Importance of Finding the Right Program

"Then this group started up in a church two townships away," she continues. "It was an adult day-care program for the frail elderly. It was run by a social worker. It had an activities director. There was one volunteer for every two or three clients. It was designed to meet the needs of individuals who required a structured environment and some assistance, but were too independent for nursing home placement. If Pop had to go to the bathroom, one of the volunteers would escort him to the john and wait outside for him. He was getting all this attention, *and it was perfect.*

"We had not realized that the senior centers were not for

him," she explains. "He needed a group designed to meet the needs of the frail elderly. Eventually, the church got a bus and driver and could pick Pop up, so I no longer had to drive back and forth to the center daily. Pop was now taken care of weekdays, from one to four. It was wonderful for him. For me, it was a blessing."

Finding the day-care center opened doors to other supportive services. "What do you do when you have a wedding to attend, and you can't leave your father at home?" Sharon asked the center's director. "What do you do when you want to drive your child to her first day of college and you need someone to stay with your father?" The Staymans learned about a help registry run by the church, which maintained a list of responsible caregivers, a number of whom were willing to stay overnight. "Pop didn't much like the idea of being left with a stranger. But eventually he complained less, and we turned to the registry more. It wasn't cheap, but it was a godsend."

Making contact with a reliable agency, hiring people who are willing and able to relieve the supercaregiver when necessary, is essential, not extravagant. The edict that "family takes care of family" should not require of family members who subscribe to it that they do it alone.

The center also offered weekly support groups for caregivers. "We really needed that at the time," says Sharon.

Joel explains, "Pop suffered a number of ministrokes, or TIAs [transient ischemic attacks]. He became very distrustful and difficult to deal with. There were constant questions from him about his finances, which I'd managed for years, keeping scrupulous records of each and every transaction. Now he took to asking repeatedly, 'What is the balance?' I would tell him. Then, as soon as Sharon and I were out of

the house, Pop would ask Dena to look at the bank statement and read him the balance. He was checking up. I didn't
appreciate it."

"We needed to talk to other people, and the support
group met that need," says Sharon. "Joel did not want to attend at first. He soon became one of the group's most eloquent members. Hearing other people express similar
feelings, learning how they dealt with comparable problems,
was good for us."

She offers an example. "My father-in-law had taken to ac-
cusing me of trying to save money by serving him second-
rate chicken and Cheerios rejects! How could he think that,
after all I'd done for him. I was feeling angry and frustrated
and brought this up in the group one evening. Another
member, the daughter of a woman who has Alzheimer's disease, turned to me and said, 'I understand how you feel.
When my mother accused me of stealing her jewelry, I felt
ready to ship her to a nursing home. Then someone suggested that I separate the speaker from the speech, that I realize that it isn't my mother who is making the accusation,
but the illness that is making her say such irrational things.
That way of thinking works for me most of the time. Maybe
it will help you to cope, too.' Her suggestion really helped
me. After all, I could not take my father-in-law's illness per-
sonally."

Support groups are important sources of emotional and
practical help for most caregivers. In his book *How We Die*,
Dr. Sherwin B. Nuland writes of such groups, "There is
strength in numbers, even when the numbers are only one
or two people who can soften the anguish by the simple act
of listening."

Like Joel, however, many people come into support

groups unsure and embarrassed, feeling that they're telling on a loved one or "airing their linen in public." The more appropriate image, I suggest, is that of the old-fashioned quilting bee in which friends sit around, swap stories, and simply are there for each other. (For what to look for in a support group, see page 54.)

In his eighty-fifth year, Ben Stayman suffered a major stroke that rendered him speechless, disoriented, and incontinent. His care could no longer be managed at home. This time the old man went from the hospital to a nursing home where, every day of the seven weeks remaining to his life, he was visited by Sharon and Joel and, often, their children, who had come to say good-bye.

"They, too, had been caregivers," says their mother, "and it wasn't a wholly negative experience. Our children learned a lesson of life that will stand them in good stead for their own lives. They are more empathic. I can't see them not being there for us if ever we need them."

"I hope and pray that it won't be necessary," says Joel.

But that was *our* parents' prayer, too.

The issue of what we do for our ailing parents, and questions of why we do it, are linked to the highly complex emotional relationships that exist between parents and children, emotions that (by the time a parent ages) are layered with history. When Joel Stayman is asked to describe the father he knew in his childhood, he talks about a man who was stinting in his praise, who lived two blocks from a major ballpark but never took his young son to a game. "In essence, he and I did not have a close relationship," he says.

Why, then, did Joel open his home to his father? Why did he agree to a situation that led to so much upheaval in the life of his own family, that caused so much stress? Did he view this as an opportunity to earn his father's praise? Did he aspire, by his actions, to be seen as the worthier son? His own explanation is far less complicated: "I did it because I had no choice. The man was my father. I did what was right."

The heart has its reasons. Sons and daughters often find caregiving easier, however, if they examine their feelings and understand what those reasons are. Nadine, the next super-caregiver we meet, has given a good deal of thought to the question of motivation. As her story makes clear, attitude makes all the difference in how, and why, she has been able to cope.

Meet Nadine

"There is an empty space in my heart," says Nadine by way of explaining the decision she came to, a year ago, to provide care for her mother, Berta. The void has existed since the day, eight years earlier, when her husband, Ralph, was diagnosed as having pancreatic cancer. He died quickly. "I don't think I'm ready yet to lose another person I love," Nadine says, speaking of her eighty-six-year-old mother, a woman whose grasp on reality is precarious at best.

Berta doesn't always remember to turn the gas off. She's forever losing her keys. She spends her days looking for misplaced items, both real and recalled from her past, growing agitated by the search and upset by her own confusion. She has fallen several times. Now that the caregiving parent has become the one who needs to be cared for, Nadine remains firm of focus: "I need to have my mother in my life, and I will do my best to help her function as well as possible."

Two years ago, Nadine was in a serious automobile accident. That brush with death made her want, more than ever, to stay close to everyone she held dear. At least once each week thereafter, Nadine would find herself driving the four-hour round-trip to see her mother, sometimes staying over until the next morning. It was a physically taxing and emotionally exhausting visit. Nadine is not an only child, and her relationship with both of her brothers is a loving one. They, too, visited their mother, although not as frequently or regularly as their sister would have liked. Mom needed more care, she told them, and decided, like the little red hen in the nursery tale, that she would have to do it herself . . . and she did.

But not immediately. First she considered alternative measures. "I thought about having Mom move to a senior residence near me," she says, "and I went to look at the kinds of places that were available. I had no idea how we would afford the move; first, I wanted to find out what there was."

The investigation was not successful. None of the residences seemed right. "Mom needed more care than she'd get in an independent living facility, but she wasn't so impaired that she required the services of a nursing home, where residents sat around in wheelchairs. At one place that came highly recommended, I was shown a room for two with a bathroom down the hall. It was extremely orderly. I was told that my mother would be permitted to bring with her only six changes of clothing and some favorite photographs, preferably framed inexpensively. ('Things have a way of disappearing around here,' said the director of admissions.)

That very day, I went home, cleared out a closet, and made room for my mother and whatever belongings and mementos she chose to bring. Two months later, she came to live with me."

For now, Nadine feels that she is able to care for her mother, with some help. Three mornings a week, Berta is kept busy at a special day-care program for persons with dementia—ironically, it is housed in the same nursing home that Nadine had seen and rejected. Friday evenings are generally spent with Nadine's daughter (Berta's granddaughter) and her family, who live in the area. The great-grandchildren provide Berta with a special kind of joy. Nadine's neighbors volunteer to stay with the older woman when Nadine has appointments to keep. Her friends accept the fact that Nadine now comes as a couple. "Grandma" is always included in their invitations to the daughter.

The arrangement isn't perfect, but it's working.

"Having my mother here is not an unmixed blessing," Nadine concedes. "There *are* times when I'd prefer just to be with my friends, evenings when I'd like to be able to sit through a dinner without worrying about whether Mom's food needs to be cut, without checking to see if she's using her napkin.

"More than a few times I have found myself wondering if, in fact, I've taken on more than I can handle. Once, Mom put water on to boil, then forgot about it and lay down for a nap. Luckily, I was in my room going over my accounts when I smelled something burning. I rushed in and turned off the gas. Now that was a dangerous thing, but there are other, petty things that wear at me. I sometimes find myself getting upset in a way that is all out of proportion to the event."

For example?

"For example, whenever I'm on the phone, my mother will call out, 'Who is it? Who are you talking to?'—not just once, but several times. I mean, that happens *every* time, and it can rattle me. But what really got to me was an incident that happened one day at the mall. My mother has a habit of wandering off, as we all do when we're attracted by different displays of merchandise, except that I begin to panic whenever I can't see her. I worry that she'll be lost and confused. On the afternoon in question, I continually had to admonish Mom to stay close, to no avail. Finally my patience wore thin and I snapped, 'Mom, come here!' Observing us, a fellow shopper remarked, 'I wish *I* had a mother to go shopping with me.' At that point, I just broke down and cried."

All in all, however, Nadine is clear that her decision was the right one for her to make. "I feel better when Mom is with me—knowing that she's clean and fed, knowing that she's okay—than I did when we lived apart. Then I was constantly worrying about her safety. Now I don't live with that worry . . . most of the time."

So *that's* the bottom line here. This is no tale of martyrdom. In taking care of her mother, and in reaching out to friends and to community programs to help in the effort, Nadine is also taking care of herself.

She keeps the nursing home brochures on file, just in case.

There are many reasons for becoming a supercaregiver. Most often, they have to do with the frailty of the parent, the severity of a health condition that precludes self-care, the economic situation (the parent or caregiver may be financially unable to afford round-the-clock home health aides or geriatric case managers, yet may have too much money to qualify for Medicaid assistance), and, as we have seen, there are the emotional ties. A further impetus for superinvolvement is cultural.

I am reminded of a young African-American woman whom I encountered at an informational meeting about nursing home placement. After years of struggle to provide the care needed by her father, whose diabetes had claimed one leg and was now affecting his kidneys, the daughter had reluctantly concluded that she would have to seek placement for him. She began to cry. "I'm going against my heart, and I'm going against my culture," she said. "I don't know how I will be able to explain this decision to the people in my church." Culture determines the caregiving role for many adult children. Within that role, however, there can still be many variations.

Meet Maryanna

"Italian mothers live with their daughters. That's the way it's always been in our culture; that's what has to be," says Maryanna, an Italian daughter, resignedly. Thirty-eight years old, divorced, and dependent on her job as a legal secretary, Maryanna is a "good daughter."

"Being good," as Maryanna sees it, means taking personal days off from work to escort her mother, Sylvia, who has breast cancer and arthritis, to medical checkups. "Being good" means rushing home after work in time to relieve the next-door neighbor who, thank the Lord, looks after her mother during the day, and whose assistance Sylvia accepted only after much coaxing and impassioned pleading by her children. (Maryanna has an older sister, Carla, who has a husband, four children, and lives in a neighboring state.) But Sylvia will not permit the neighbor to do any cleaning or laundry. "I'm not crippled; I'm still able to take care of my own home," she insists, which means, in effect, that the work is left for Maryanna.

"Being good" means that Maryanna spends weekends tending to her mother—cooking, cleaning, playing the piano for her. Her mother will not accept substitute care when she knows that her daughter is available. "Being good" means bundling her mother up and getting her to church on Sundays, rain or shine, where the priest and parishioners tell Maryanna, every week, what a very good daughter she is. Ask Maryanna about the last movie she has seen, and she cannot remember, it has been that long. Her last leisurely meal out with friends? It was a lunchtime celebration for one of her coworkers. "What do I do for relaxation?" she asks. "I watch television and drink a lot of wine."

Among the ranks of supercaregivers we find many adult children, like Maryanna, who are so keenly attuned to the needs of their parents, and so dedicated to meeting them, that they lose sight of their own lives, their own requirements, in the process often becoming depressed, distressed, and drained of energy. They get an A in caring for others, an F in self-care. In the words of noted gerontologist Robert Butler, they become "the second patient."

Gail Hoffmann, associate in counseling at the Alzheimer's Association, New York City chapter, tells me about supercaregivers, like Maryanna, who give their all for their ailing parents, taking little or no time for themselves. "They rush home from work instead of meeting a friend for a drink.

They pay a caregiver but feel they have to supervise the caregiver constantly. They justify their total absorption in the aged parent by explaining it as a personal debt that is now being paid. 'My mother was always there for me; now it's my turn to be there for her,' they will tell me. I hear that a lot from people. 'Yes,' I respond, 'but your mother took a break! And so should you.'"

"Why should a parent accept household help or a hired caregiver when a daughter/son/niece/sister is always available, when the family member comes by daily and phones several times, morning and afternoon?" asks Fern Parker, coordinator of group activities and respite programs for The Brookdale Center on Aging. Parker recommends that family caregivers who are faced with this situation reduce the visits and phone calls, encouraging the patient to understand that she does require outside help. "But the daughter/son/niece then has to have the courage not to stop by, not to call back," says Parker, "and that takes time."

It is, in fact, possible for adult children to repay their personal debt to parents without bankrupting their own lives. Stephan, whom we meet next, is a supercaregiver who invested time, energy, and devotion in his parents' care, who also located help for them when it was needed, and who reaped incalculable personal rewards in the process.

Meet Stephan

Caregiver extraordinaire. These two words enter my mind and remain there as I listen to Stephan Moore, a fifty-three-year-old engineer, describe the course of his mother Kathleen's eleven-year struggle with heart disease and provide a detailed account of the measures he took to address her many needs and improve the quality of her life.

Stephan is a doer whose approaches to work and life are one and the same: identify the problem, research possible solutions, implement the best plan. As quickly becomes apparent, he was also a most loving son. "I came late into my parents' lives, and was very close to them, although they were quite opposite in character," he says. "My father, Frank, was negative and withholding; my mother was very positive and supportive. She encouraged me in everything. Eventually, it became my turn to do the same for her."

Stephan remembers his mother as having a number of problems, mostly stress-related, that over the years required medical attention. They were not a matter of real concern. The more serious changes, when they came, were barely noticed. Stephan observed his mother experiencing some shortness of breath after climbing the stairs or being out in the cold. He suggested that she get a checkup and made an appointment for her with his own cardiologist, who diagnosed angina, put Kathleen on Procardia (one of the blocker drugs), and prescribed a number of other heart drugs.

Recognizing that his mother's activities were likely to be limited for a while, Stephan next set about addressing Kathleen's emotional need to feel, and be, useful. "My mother used to crochet wonderful little animals for her friends to give to their grandchildren," he says. "I brought some samples of her handiwork to the attention of a crafts-shop owner, who bought them and asked for more. They'd send her wool via UPS; she'd make half a dozen animals a week, and I'd bring them in to the store. They'd send her checks.

Mom was delighted. This arrangement went on for about ten years."

Kathleen Moore experienced several heart attacks and arrhythmias, followed by a mild stroke, which left her without speech for a short period. "That was the beginning of my *total* involvement in her care," says her son, going on to describe just what that entailed.

"I had developed a friendly relationship with a social worker at one of the hospitals that had treated Mom. She told me about a visiting nurse service run by the hospital. For a nominal fee, I could arrange to have a licensed nurse come by my parents' home once or twice a week to check my mother's blood pressure and medications, and generally see that she was receiving proper care. I signed on for the service."

Managing Multiple Medications

"My father was bewildered by all of this and would often forget to give Mom her medication or to get straight which ones she was to take, and when. There were many medications at this time, and they were often being changed. To help my parents keep track, I developed a chart, flat like a board, where I arranged little boxes. I'd phone Mom every morning, and we'd set up the chart: how many pills she was to take, how many times a day. When necessary, I could get other people to check it. (I had all the information on my computer, so every time my mother's medications were changed, I could redo the chart.) This became a tool that we used for the next five years. It seemed to simplify things a lot.

"Next, I had to find a local medical resource. Mom could

no longer easily make the trip to Manhattan, where I live, from the Bronx, where she and my father lived, so I needed to find a heart specialist nearer her home. My doctor suggested that I phone the biggest hospital in my parents' area and ask for a list of cardiologists on their staff. They sent me names and addresses of sixteen doctors. Using a map of the area, I checked off several whose offices were relatively close to my parents' address. My doctor chose one who seemed to have the best credentials. When I learned that the physician we'd settled on also had office hours on Thursday evenings, I was elated. So it became a ritual. Every Thursday night, I would drive to the Bronx, take Mom to her doctor, and spend time with the folks. Eventually, we hit upon the right mixture of medications, and Mom started to get stronger."

Just as life was becoming manageable, Stephan's father— the healthy parent—suffered a massive brain hemorrhage, and died within a week. "Afterward, I'd find myself phoning my mother three, four times a day to check on her welfare. This caused a certain amount of conflict in my own home. I had a tendency to want to spend more time, more effort, with my mother, and my wife said, 'You can't go overboard.' She was very helpful and supportive with my mom, but she had a different perspective.

"If I was to be less anxious, I knew that I could not have my mother living alone in a place that I couldn't get to easily. I told Mom that we'd have to think about how she would live. There seemed to be three choices: she could go to a senior residence (she was adamantly opposed); she could come live with us (I would have liked that, but my wife was not in accord, and I knew better than to press the issue); or she could move to an apartment closer to us (she seemed amenable to that). So I found her a light, airy studio apartment, set it up, and my mother moved in.

"Then I enrolled her in Lifeline, a service that provided her with a transmitter, to be worn around the neck, that she could activate to reach an emergency phone number and summon help. Having my mother wear it was reassuring to me."

Lifeline is but one of many personal emergency response systems that are available to the elderly and disabled. Some rely on transmitters worn by the individual; in others, devices are placed in the bedroom or bathroom. These systems are particularly useful for people who live alone, providing elders and their caregivers with a sense of security. A word of advice, based on some anxious moments in my own family: Lifeline doesn't work if the transmitter is left on the bedside table and the patient suffers a fall while heading toward the bathroom. It's not enough to just arrange for the system; the importance of having the at-risk parent wear it *at all times* must also be stressed.

More Resources . . .

"I returned to the notion of finding ways of getting my mother involved with people," Stephan continues, "and asked my assistant to check out all of the agencies that offer services to the aged, then let me know what those services are. One agency offered a friendly visitor program that matches the elderly with a younger person who will stop in and do whatever a friend might do: play Scrabble, write letters, or simply sit and talk. Mom's visitor was a lovely young woman in her twenties who became a friend. My mother liked to entertain, so I'd arrange for food to be delivered to her home and Mom would prepare dinner for the two of them. Frequently, my family would come by for dinner, too. It gave my mother a real life instead of just an existence.

"I was also told about a hospital-managed outreach program for the elderly that provides social activities for participants as well as monitoring their health care. I arranged to have Mom interviewed. *Just as she had taken me for an interview for kindergarten, I now took her and hoped she would do well.* She was accepted into the program, and was given the choice of attending two or three sessions a week, from ten o'clock to three.

"How would she get there? They suggested that I contact Access-A-Ride, a publicly funded service that provides safe transportation, at a nominal fee, to people with disabilities. I applied. Once the application was accepted, my mother was placed on a waiting list, and was serviced on an as-available basis. Later she became a regular, and they established a schedule to take her to and from the outreach program."

[About transportation services: The federal government, under the Older Americans Act, has mandated the provision of transportation services in response to the need of older and disabled persons for mobility—to get to a congregate meal, visit a doctor, or do local errands. These programs, with names like Dial-A-Ride and Dial-A-Car, are found in many areas of the country. Transportation services are also available through churches and various neighborhood programs. A phone call to your Area Agency on Aging office will provide information about transportation services in your community. Calls to the services will provide you with information on how to apply.

If you live in a community that has a mass-transit system, door-to-door transportation for people with disabilities may be provided under the Americans with Disabilities Act. Contact your local mass-transit system for information on availability and application procedures.]

"So," Stephan says with evident satisfaction, "all of a sudden my mother, this virtual shut-in, was on her own, able to take transportation, attend a program, teach others in the program how to do crafts, come home, and entertain guests. It was the most amazing transformation. There was quality to my mother's life until the day her heart finally gave out, a year and a half later."

Caring for Oneself—the "Whys" of the Caregiver Extraordinaire

Stephan explains his extraordinary involvement in his mother's care, his seemingly selfless devotion, in this way: "There were two things that were operating in me. First, very selfishly, *I was trying to preserve my own life.* I had a business to run. I was not about to sacrifice that. I had a certain kind of lifestyle, a family lifestyle. I was not about to sacrifice that, either. And a certain kind of freedom. My wife and I did a fair amount of traveling throughout this time, when I would make sure that there was someone to look in on my mother. So I was trying to create some structure that would allow my mother to do what she did well. I had the idea that if I could get Mom more involved with people, then *I* would have a lot of freedom. And it worked. *I knew that getting organized, getting in control, was better than not being in con-*

trol and being at the mercy of my mother's illness. If I could deal with issues of health and security (which included having her close by so I could drop in when I needed to), and if I could get her a structure so that she wouldn't be a lonely, needy, elderly person who would be constantly looking to me to provide companionship, then I could continue with my life as I wanted to.

"Then there was this tremendous debt that I felt I had to repay. I don't know how to be specific about it, but my mother had really allowed me to be what I am, so I felt that a payback was required and I wanted to do that. The time that I devoted to my mother's care in those final years was extremely important in my life, and I really made an effort to make the most of it. I don't know why it worked out this way, but it gave me an opportunity to reach closure, to find great peace."

In summary, then, here's what helped the supercaregivers:

- having the support of family and friends;
- keeping a sense of perspective—knowing why they were involved;
- making time for themselves (for both business and leisure);
- asking for help when needed;
- becoming organized;
- utilizing social work services;
- introducing in-home care;
- finding a suitable adult day-care program;
- employing a personal emergency response system;
- enlisting the support of friendly visitor programs;

- arranging for transportation services;
- joining a support group.

The following chapter discusses three of the concrete aids listed above—support groups, adult day-care centers, and in-home care—and shows caregivers how they can help themselves and their parents by finding and utilizing the appropriate resource.

CHAPTER 2

HELPING YOURSELF AND HELPING YOUR PARENT

I. THE SUPPORT GROUP

The ways in which we manage to care *for* our parents and the feelings we bring to caring *about* them are highly personal. When a mother or father shows signs of failing, each son or daughter has to determine how to deal with the new situation and how to adjust to a new status: caregiver. Each of us feels very much alone.

We suddenly find ourselves burdened by chores and bewildered by choices. Can Mom be left alone? Should we start looking into an elder residence? How does one go about finding an aide or selecting an institution? How much will help cost? Can we afford it? Are we seeing the right doctor? Is the parent receiving appropriate medication? Questions come up day by day, sometimes hour by hour, as the situation changes. *We need to have good, detailed, timely information.*

We find ourselves overwhelmed by our feelings, as well: feelings of guilt, love, anger, impatience, inadequacy, selflessness, self-interest. We question what we're doing and what we're *not* doing. Are we making the right decisions? Are we right in leaving decision making to others? *We need to be able to talk about our emotions and insecurities.*

We need a support group.

Caregiver support groups are important sources of practical and emotional help. "Attending a support group placed things in perspective for my sister and me and gave us some direction," says Polly, a forty-six-year-old daughter whose mother is undergoing chemotherapy treatment following surgery for sarcoma of the uterus. "The social worker immediately set the tone, which really helped. She told us, 'You can't predict how your mother will react to the treatment or how effective it will be, so your day-to-day has no track. Anticipating what your next experience will be is not productive. You just have to wait and see and decide at the moment.

"'Still, there *are* things you can do ahead of time,' she said. 'You can make contact with agencies and inquire about hiring aides to be with your mother if she needs them; you can learn about organizations, like Cancer Care, that offer information, counseling, and assistance to patients and caregivers.' One of the support group members told us about a shop where we could find wigs at reasonable prices. She'd used it for her own mother. 'The owner is very sensitive,' she said. We hadn't considered the possibility that Mom would need a wig. That's the first thing the support group did for us. It gave us understanding and direction."

For Gerald, who is helping to manage the care of his seventy-one-year-old mother, who has Alzheimer's, the support group he attends twice each month has become "an anchor." At forty-three, Gerald is one of the youngest members of his group, which includes adult children, siblings of the patient, and spouses. About a third are male, two thirds are female. The coordinator is a psychiatric social worker.

"The group has provided me with emotional and practical support in situations where I've run into a wall over how to get things done," says Gerald. He offers an example. "My mother got to the point where she needed help at home, but she vigorously resisted it. She'd become agitated at the mention of a housekeeper, and she refused to have anyone who even looked like hired help enter her house. She sent two perfectly nice women away. My father has his own health problems, and I couldn't keep taking time from work and my family to look in on the two of them.

"When I spoke about this problem at one of our meetings, the group members came up with the idea that I introduce the home aide as a friend and have my mother slowly get used to her. So that's what I did. One Wednesday evening, we had a dinner party. The guests included my aunt (my mother's sister), two of her daughters, and this very nice woman who was introduced as the friend of one of my cousins. The next week, the woman came for coffee, and stayed for two hours. Now she comes three afternoons a week. And the funny thing is, my mother accepts her. It was a suggestion I never would have thought of, and it worked!

"There's a lot of practical support, and there's a lot of emotional support in the group," says Gerald. "There's a lot of pain there, and a lot of humor, too. I can't tell you how much I look forward to those meetings. They're a lifesaver."

People come to support groups for many reasons. Some, like Polly, come when they first learn about a parent's disease or condition. Others, like Sharon and Joel Stayman (whom we met in the previous chapter), come because the pressures of caregiving have become too great to bear alone. And still others come seeking information and support around a difficult decision, like whether to place a parent in a nursing home. They stay on when they discover, like Gerald, that the group can serve as an anchor in some very choppy waters.

Rea Kahn, a longtime coordinator of support groups for the Alzheimer's Association, offers a similar comparison. "The support group can be a life preserver for many caregivers," she says. "It serves many purposes. It can provide information—about the disease, about resources, about what to expect, about coping mechanisms.

"But what I find, and what I respect so much, is what I call *the magical curative power of the group.*" She explains, "When you put a group of people in a room week after week after week, their emotional feelings come to the surface and they are amplified by bouncing off one another in this room. If we are talking about a topic, even if we are talking about a concrete issue, sooner or later our feelings will start to surface toward each other, toward the material. It's exactly those feelings that are curative for the individuals in that group.

"With the direction of a trained leader, those feelings can become more manageable. You can normalize them for this situation. For example, if I am outside this community and I tell anyone, 'I had such strong feelings, I wanted to kill my father,' people will look at me and be stunned. But in the support group, everybody understands that language. They understand the feelings of wanting the situation to come to an end, and at the same time giving your father exquisite care. And I think that is another function of the group, to normalize the very potent feelings that are uncomfortable for most of us. It doesn't take the feelings away, but the universality of the experience is one of the reasons that the group becomes therapeutic.

"Another function of the group," Kahn continues, "is that it cuts down on the isolation that a caregiver feels. Someone once said to me, 'We're all in the same ocean, but we're all in different boats.' I love that image because *everyone's situation is unique*, the patient's experience as well as the caregiver's. The relationship with the parent is different, the finances, the aides. But I have a sense that we *are* all in the same ocean. And I think that a good support group allows the differences to surface at the same time that it recognizes the similarities."

There is great variety in the makeup of support groups:

- some are closed, maintaining the makeup and integrity of the original group, while others are open and accommodate drop-ins;
- some are narrowly limited (daughters of Alzheimer's patients; male spouse caregivers), while others are more broadly defined (available to anyone caring for an aging relative);

- some meet weekly, while others meet monthly;
- some are led by a professional, while others are self-directed;
- some have a sponsoring organization, while others take place in members' homes.

I believe in support groups. In a different context I have been both a member and a leader of such groups, and have seen firsthand how effective they can be. I have witnessed the wonder on people's faces when they enter a group for the first time and discover that they are not alone, that others are challenged by the same problems and feel many of the same feelings. I have remarked on the relief that comes over people when they find that here, in this place, it is okay for them to speak the unspeakable. And I have seen strength come to those who, in learning from others, were helped to find new ways through the caregiving wilderness.

A good support group does many things:

- it provides information on the illness, including how to manage it;
- it helps combat the stigma of the illness;
- it permits you to say things that you would not have the courage to admit elsewhere for fear of being judged. When people in support groups say, "I know what you're going through," the chances are they do, and they will not judge you;
- it allows you to laugh, even though much of the laughter may be black humor;
- it relieves stress;

- it provides some perspective—you may discover that your problem is not as bad as you thought *or* that you've taken too much on and help is required.

The earlier you become involved in a support group, the better. On the other hand, it is never too late to reach out. Whatever brings you in is fine.

The Wrong Way to Choose a Group: A Personal Experience

When I learned the nature of my mother's illness, I was upset, confused, and ignorant of what to expect. I held long-distance phone conversations with my sister and brother during the day, and cried into my pillow at night. I didn't get much work done. In search of some direction, I placed a telephone call to the Alzheimer's Association and inquired about the existence of support groups.

What I did next could serve as a case history of how *not* to go about locating an appropriate support group. Steps one and two were correct: I contacted an appropriate organization and spoke with a knowledgeable staff member. In fact, I was directed to Rea Kahn. She was not in, and so I left a message. That evening, she phoned me from her home.

She asked me to describe my situation and needs, then suggested a group, made up mostly of daughters. But the group met on weekday afternoons, and I told her that my schedule could more easily accommodate an evening meeting. Rea then mentioned another group, one that met in a location across town. I'd rather have something closer to home, I said. (Looking back, I don't know why she put up with me.) Well, Rea said with some hesitation, there was another group; it met within walking distance of my home, on Wednesday evenings, but it was probably the wrong group for me. I said I'd try it.

I arrived at my first meeting. The group had gathered in a cozy apartment, the home of one of its members. Men and women of mostly late middle age entered, embraced one another, and quickly took their seats in chairs that had been arranged in a semicircle. After introducing me briefly, the group facilitator quickly turned to one of the members, and asked if he'd like to share with the group the events of the week just past. It had been a rough week, said the man, explaining that his wife was found wandering one night at some distance from their home. She had let herself out while he slept. Fortunately, she was wearing an identity bracelet, enabling the police to bring her home. That very day, her husband told us, he had internal locks placed on the door to his home, and hoped that they would do the trick.

[About the identity bracelet: The Alzheimer's Association Safe Return program helps identify, locate, and return individuals who are memory-impaired due to Alzheimer's disease or a related disorder. The program provides: an identity bracelet or necklace; clothing labels and wallet cards that identify the individual; registration in a national database; a twenty-four-hour toll-free number to contact when an individual is lost or found. If wandering is a problem for your parent, you will want to contact the Association to learn more about this program.]

The group members offered words of encouragement to the speaker. Someone asked whether he had tried hanging bells on the doorknob before bedtime, the better to alert him if his wife again attempted to wander out at night. The empathy, the concern found in that warm room, bespoke a kind of intimacy that exists among good friends or family members who have been through a lot together. I felt like the visitor who came to dinner.

Moreover, I quickly discovered, most of the group members were spouses who were the primary caregivers to a husband or wife who was far along in the course of this devastating disease. How could I tell these good people, who now changed the diapers of partners with whom they had often made love, that I was concerned because my mother kept misplacing her keys? I was at the beginning of the journey through this illness; they were in a different and, for me, scary place. I did not stay for coffee.

The second support group I attended met on a weekday morning. I had to take two buses to get there, but it was a group comprised entirely of women, daughters, and granddaughters, and so I felt—for the first several weeks—that this was where I belonged. We all told our stories. And the next week we told them again. Then again. We became stuck in our stories, each of us a soloist, when support and blending were called for. The group facilitator lacked the skills to help us help each other. We did not move forward. It wasn't long before the group fell apart.

Instead of seeking a third support group, I have settled on attending some of the monthly meetings run by the Association. There I can ask my questions and receive information that I need in order to help me make important care decisions for my mother. I am comfortable in doing research, in finding answers to questions, and so this helps me feel better. What's missing, however, is the emotional connection. I know I must do something about that soon.

What to Look for in a Support Group

But this time I want to do it right, so I admit the error of my ways and go back to Rea Kahn to find out: "What should someone look for in a support group?" The suggestions and observations that follow are hers.

1. Before you attend a group, be sure that you have some knowledge about what the group is like and who is in the group. [Had I known, for example, that the first group I attended was made up of spouse caregivers, I would not have attended.]

2. Look for a group where the leader is trained in group work and is knowledgeable about the disease that they're working with. While there is much to be said for self-help groups whose members share coping mechanisms, I find that, often, without direction, a group will go awry. Conflicts will come up, and if there's no one with skills to mediate the controversy, then you have a revolving-door policy where people come, stay a little while, get a little uncomfortable, and move out. A good group, in my mind, is a cohesive group, where the members find the attachment to the group attractive. There's a sense of community, a commitment to one another.

3. Inquire into the frequency of meetings. The more often a group meets, the more cohesive it's going to be.

4. Once you attend a group, trust your intuitive feelings about what you experience there. If it feels wrong to you, look elsewhere.

"Support groups are not for everyone," she concludes. "Some caregivers who are in crisis may do better if they see someone individually, and work on the issues that are troubling them. Other caregivers find family counseling more helpful."

Joining a support group is not an entry to easy answers. It is a process. There is little question in my mind that, for most caregivers, it is a process that is worth entering into.

How to Locate a Caregiver Support Group

There are many ways to locate a support group. A good first step is to contact an organization that deals specifically with the illness or condition in question. Groups like the American Diabetes Association, American Parkinson's Disease Foundation, American Cancer Society, and American Heart Association will send you information on the illness and direct you to local chapters that are likely to offer support groups. You can find these organizations in your local telephone book or by calling the 800-number information directory service.

Another good way to proceed is to contact the local municipal office on aging and ask for direction.

Self-help clearinghouses, found in many communities, will refer you to support groups in your area. They, too, are listed in your telephone directory. If not, check with Information to see if there is a self-help clearinghouse number in your area.

An organization called Children of Aging Parents (CAPS) provides a national directory of support groups for caregivers of the elderly. They can be reached at (215) 945-6900.

Local hospitals, religious institutions, community centers, geriatric homes, and adult day-care centers often sponsor support groups for caregivers to the frail elderly. Begin by phoning one or two; if they do not have a group, the chances are good that they will be able to direct you to services in your community. Networking is a very effective method of obtaining the information you need.

II. THE ADULT DAY-CARE CENTER

> *Then this group started up in a church two townships away. It was an adult day-care program for the frail elderly. . . . It was a blessing.*
>
> —SHARON STAYMAN, CAREGIVER

One of the most heartening developments in caring for the elderly in recent years has been the enormous growth in adult day-care centers, which offer support, supervision, and specialized services to older men and women who are physically disabled or mentally impaired, and provide respite for their caregivers. Approximately 3,000 programs exist nationwide. Many are affiliated with larger organizations such as nursing homes, hospitals, religious institutions, and multipurpose senior centers. Most operate on a nonprofit basis.

The term "day care" is an unfortunate choice, I feel, because it perpetuates the comparison of frail elders with dependent children. Terminology aside, the day-care (or adult treatment) center is one of the most helpful resources to benefit the elderly person who is receiving care and the adult child or other individual who is responsible for providing the care.

Why a Specialized Day-Care Program?

People with mental and physical disabilities are unwelcome at most senior centers and, if accepted by the administration, are frequently shunned by the group's more able participants. I speak of this from personal observation. When my mother was an independent senior, sound of mind and body, she was a "regular" at a center near her home. She performed in holiday entertainments, proudly reciting the lines she'd been given to memorize. She bought tickets to fund-raising events and was even secretary of her group for a while.

Time passed. Mom began to grow confused. The more she forgot to return phone calls and failed to remember meetings, the more friends fell away. Older people tend to flee from dementia (and those who suffer from it) as from the plague. Additionally, the same center staff that used to warmly greet the well Rebecca became less welcoming when her memory began to fail. My mother ventured out to the senior center less and less frequently. Nobody phoned to find out how, and where, she was. Nobody stopped by. Like Ben Stayman, whose physical infirmities called for a specially designed response (see chapter 1), Mom needed a place and program specifically suited to her needs.

That I took so long in finding that program is attributable to two factors—one personal, the other practical. Let's consider the personal first, for I find evidence daily that the reasoning behind my own reluctance to act is a judgment that prevents many caregivers from seeking appropriate help and many elders from enjoying the benefits to be found in a well-designed and -implemented day-care program.

Very simply, I wanted my mother to continue to attend

the regular program at her neighborhood senior center because I did not wish to admit to myself the extent of her impairment. I didn't know anything about the kind of population I might find in a day-care program, but I was sure that my mother wasn't so bad off that she belonged there . . . not yet.

I am not alone in this self-deception. The other day, I spoke with a man weighed down by caring for his sixty-six-year-old wife, Lynn, once a successful clinical psychologist. She still recognizes the name "Freud," her husband tells me, but she's no longer able to remember his theories. The husband spoke of the pressures on him of trying to rush home from work, several days a week, in order to have lunch with his wife. "She's always been such a social person," he said, "and now she is so alone." I asked if he had investigated day care. "Lynn won't accept it," he replied, abruptly dismissing the idea. "She says those programs are for old people, and she's not old." Was it the caregiver or patient who protested too much?

I have visited many day-care programs. To my surprise (and dismay), the men and women I met there were not the oldest of the old, nor were they necessarily the most dependent. Day-care users range in age from men and women in their fifties and sixties to those who are a good deal further along in years. They engage in a variety of activities: some play cards, others play lightweight versions of bowling or horseshoes, some cook, others do carpentry, some play the piano, and most join in singalongs. They sit down to lunch together.

Robert Butler, M.D., author of the Pulitzer Prize–winning book *Why Survive? Being Old in America*, is a strong proponent of day treatment programs. "Most of the cutting-edge thinking is that we have to move toward day-care centers (or what I call family service centers) where people go to get services rather than being served at home or in institutions," Dr. Butler says. "The problem with people being at home is that there is no socialization, no assurance of how well they are taken care of by home care workers, no guarantee of hot meals, and no annual flu shots."

I began to look into a day-care program for my mother by phoning the local office of aging, which provided me with a list of centers and sponsoring organizations in her area. That's when I ran into a practical barrier: all of the centers I contacted were oversubscribed. If this is the situation that you, too, confront, ask to have your parent's name placed on a waiting list. Then ask for leads to other programs. Make one call after another. Be persistent. In this way, I learned of two programs so new that they had not yet been listed with the office of aging. A phone call to one resulted in an invitation for Mom and me to visit. We accepted.

The Visit

It is a beautiful fall day. I pick my mother up, and drive with her to the nursing home in which the center is located. On the way, Mom remarks on the beauty of the changing leaves. "If only people could renew themselves like the trees," she tells me. . . . *If only*, I think.

I park the car and we approach the home. About a half dozen women and a couple of men, all in wheelchairs, are seated in a small grassy area in front of the building. A white-uniformed attendant sits with them. She is reading a newspaper. In the brightly lit, spanking-clean lobby, we're directed to the elevator. The center is located on the top floor, we are told. Mom appears fearful that we've come to sign her into care. I reassure her that we're just here to see the day program. It will be good for her, I say. Trust me. (To tell the truth, I, too, am discomfited by this view of the future, and assume a purposeful air to reassure my mother, to reassure myself.)

We take the elevator to the top floor, where sunlight illuminates the brightly painted murals that fill the walls of an attractive, spacious area. A piano sits in the corner. Outside there is a large garden terrace where, I later learn, lunchtime barbecues are held during warmer weather. Off a corridor, away from the central area, we pass rooms whose doors bear the designations "Beauty Parlor," "Podiatrist," "Rehabilitative Therapy." A good deal of care has gone into creating this cheerful, helpful environment. I am impressed.

We are greeted by the director. She takes me into her office where I learn more about the program, and am given medical and financial forms to fill out for my mother. I am told that this center is open to all adults who require supportive care because of general frailty or specific physical or neurological conditions, such as Alzheimer's, Parkinson's, and strokes. It provides a comprehensive program of health, nutritional, and social services.

I'm handed a brochure that shows a lively group of elders, well groomed and able bodied, clustered around a piano, apparently enjoying a songfest. I then glance through the glass-paneled office to the main area, where I can see that my mother has joined the group participants at a long table. A game of bingo is in progress. One of the players, a woman with a vacant but beautiful smile, gets up, begins pacing down the long corridor, and is brought back to the room, where she continues smiling and pacing. Another woman (a stroke victim, I am told) sits hunched over in her wheelchair. She's exhausted, having just returned from receiving physical therapy. There is a younger man, perhaps in his thirties, whom the director describes to me as "mentally challenged," and an agitated older man who keeps shouting "Bingo" at the top of his voice. Looking dazed, my mother turns to the recreation director and asks, "What am I doing here?"

I begin to cry. "I'm sorry," I say to the program director, handing back the application forms. "You are wonderful people, but this is not the right program for my mother." I wait until lunch is served, and drive Mom home.

I have learned several lessons this day:

• A homogeneous group is preferable to an all-inclusive elder program. People who are physically challenged but mentally alert do best in programs that challenge and entertain them within the limits of their disability. Those suffering from cognitive impairment benefit from programs that stimulate the mind and help participants stay in touch with everyday reality. Within each group, it is possible to find even further variations, based on the level of functioning of group members.

• Brochures do not tell the story. It's important for you, the caregiver, to pay an on-site visit to any program that's being considered.

• It's best to make that first visit alone, unaccompanied by the frail elderly parent. (I do think that a parent should be involved in decision making, whenever possible, but I've learned that it's best if the adult child manages the preliminary research, then shares with the parent what he or she has found.)

Some day-care centers require a completed application prior to setting up a meeting with you. In such cases, I have found it helpful to ask to speak with the director and to then explain what I am looking for in a day-care center and why I do not want to confuse my mother with visits to a variety of places. I have been politely insistent, and it has worked.

After sitting in on several programs, I finally came upon one that just felt right. The center in question operates two programs: one for patients with chronic health conditions, the other for Alzheimer's patients who are verbal and able to participate in professionally led discussions. The programs offer a full activity schedule, including music and crafts, exercise and cooking, personal care and trips within the community. There is a plan for each patient, and family members are invited to periodic conferences about the parent's adjustment and needs. Transportation and a hot lunch are included.

We applied, and were placed on a waiting list. When a spot opened up, Mom and I came for an interview. She passed! Mom now attends the center two days a week. "It's a wonderful thing that they do for the older people," she says. "It is not good to be alone."

What to Look for in a Day-Care Center

A high-quality adult day-care center:

- looks clean, smells clean, *is* clean and safe;

- conducts an assessment of individuals prior to admission to determine their range of abilities and needs;
- develops an individualized treatment plan for each participant, monitoring his or her progress on a regular basis;
- includes family members in assessment and planning;
- makes counseling available to the family;
- provides a full range of services that include recreational and educational programming, rehabilitative services, medication dispensing, and nutrition (including a midday meal);
- may also include health screening and monitoring, and such medical services as ophthalmology, dentistry, and podiatry, as well as personal care;
- employs qualified staff and makes use of well-trained volunteers (When you visit, check to see how staff members interact with clients. Do they talk down to participants? Are people treated with dignity?);
- provides transportation or refers you to a Dial-A-Ride program when such service is necessary;
- adheres to state licensure requirements, where they exist.

Funding is often a problem. Many adult day-care centers accept Medicaid reimbursements and/or set fees on a sliding scale, based on the client's ability to pay.

Most day-care programs take place on weekdays. Hours of operation vary. (For more information, write to the National Institute on Adult Daycare, 409 3rd St. S.W., Washington, DC 20024, or phone [202] 479-1200.)

Here's what I now understand: *Your parent does not have*

*to be "that bad off" to benefit from participation in an adult
day-care center.* On the days that my mother attends the day-
care program, she returns home happier and more alert. Last
week, an aide gave my mother a manicure. "It's wonderful,
what they do for the older people," Mom remarked as she
showed off her nails. My mother often forgets that she's been
to the day-care center. The manicure reminds her of where
she was.

I need no reminding. On the days that my mother goes to
the center, I find myself waking up with a smile, going about
my business with a lighter heart. For the supercaregiver, the
effect is even more dramatic. A friend of mine, a woman
with full responsibility for the care of her father, says of the
time that her parent spends at a day-care center, "It may be
for only four hours a day, but for me it's like being underwa-
ter and coming up for air. I'm able to breathe again. And I
can go on."

III. IN-HOME CARE

For a long time, longer than was reasonable, my sister,
brother, and I chose to ignore signs that our mother needed
some assistance with daily living. To begin with, there were
lapses in personal care: a button missing on a blouse, a spot
on a jacket, a hem undone—nothing, really, to worry about.
The change was notable mainly because Mom had always
been meticulous about her appearance.

Later, we began to notice that her housekeeping skills
were slipping as well. Frequently, we would turn on the
kitchen light in her home and see roaches scurry from the
bookshelves and across the linoleum floor. If any of us men-

tioned it, our mother would become indignant. "The house is clean," she'd insist. "Why are you suddenly finding fault?" It wasn't that we were on an inspection tour when we visited our mother; it was just that, well, the problems were becoming more and more obvious.

We suggested hiring someone to come in one day a week and help with housekeeping chores. After all, Mom was in her eighties; it wasn't such an outlandish idea. She bristled at the notion. "What am I, an invalid?" she demanded. "I always managed without help, and I'm still able to manage, thank God."

So we would back off for a while because we didn't want to threaten our parent's self-esteem . . . and because we didn't know how best to handle the matter. How do you impose help on someone who is adamantly opposed to it, who doesn't want a stranger to enter her home and her life? What if we hired someone and our mother then sent her away? But Mom was becoming increasingly frail and forgetful, and it was clear that something had to be done.

At the geriatric clinic, Mom's social worker advised us that the time had come for the family to stop consulting with our mother about home care and, instead, take the steps necessary to put it in place. In the doctor's judgment, our mother required assistance not just with housekeeping but with chores such as grocery shopping and cooking, as well as bathing and even getting safely from place to place. We would never arrive at the point where we all needed to be if we didn't get started. He said, "Just make sure that one of you is there the first time the homemaker arrives, to reassure your mother and to help her adjust to the new situation."

We followed his instructions, and they worked. But not right away. That first morning, I arrived in time to greet the new homemaker and show her around my mother's three-room apartment. She quickly set to work in the kitchen while Mom and I took refuge in the living room. To ease our discomfort, I kept up a constant chatter about family, friends, the day's weather, the state of the world, while my mother intoned "I don't need her" like a mantra, invoking the gods to restore her to full independence.

Little by little, Mom began to appreciate the look and feel of a clean apartment, then gradually realized that she did need help. Getting our mother to accept the presence of a stranger in her home was a breakthrough that in time became even more important, for Mom had a "silent heart attack," was put on medication, and needed even more help in order to be able to continue to live at home. We children explained that we were concerned for her safety and couldn't be there each day to see to it that her needs were being met. We stood firm.

As a result, a home-care attendant now comes in to help my mother seven days a week. Mom refers to this good woman as "my friend" (largely because she's unable to remember her care provider's name), and although my mother periodically replays her old scripts by protesting the necessity of having a home-care attendant, she does so in a half-hearted manner.

I sometimes think that one of the reasons we waited so long to get Mom the help she needed is because, like many adult children, we had difficulty in admitting that the time had come to involve others in the work of caring for our parent. For certain ethnic groups, in particular, family tradition and cultural beliefs lead sons and daughters to undertake heroic

efforts to do everything themselves, even if it means sacrific-
ing other responsibilities to family, work, and self. **Here's
what helps:** exploring the field of at-home services.

A diverse and rapidly growing industry, home care is an important alternative to institutionalization. Depending on the
needs of the patient, home care can involve: physicians, registered and practical nurses, various rehabilitation therapists,
nutritionists, social workers, aides to help with personal and
household chores, house cleaners, providers of meals and
transportation, friendly visitors.

Basically, however, there are three levels of home care
workers that caregivers ought to know about:

- *homemakers,* who provide housekeeping services
  and general cleaning. The service does not include
  personal care;
- *home health aides,* who provide personal care and
  assist with household chores, meal preparation, and
  daily living activities;
- *registered nurses,* who evaluate care, keep records
  of the patient's medications and progress, and ad-
  minister the required treatment.

Working with a Licensed Home-Care Agency

Many people who decide to seek the assistance of a home-
care aide prefer to work with a reliable home-care agency—
in essence, the family hires the agency, which employs,
trains, and supervises the aide. Caregiver Amy Sutton, who

chose this course for her father, explains, "I had heard too many stories about elder abuse, and I was very concerned that we not have someone we didn't know and who wasn't supervised. The home-care worker sent by the agency I hired is honest and dependable, a lifesaver."

Responding to the demand for services that make it possible for frail elders to remain at home, many nursing homes have added in-home services as well as adult day-care centers to the programs they offer. Ken Stevenson (see chapter 7) has found it helpful to employ a geriatric management service operated by a nursing home to oversee his mother's care.

He explains, "The home provides a continuum of services that treat people from the time they are most healthy to when they are most sick. Mom receives round-the-clock care in her own home. If one woman can't take the five o'clock shift, the agency will see to it that *someone* is there. Since I don't live around the corner, that is very valuable to me. A senior nurse periodically comes by to check on Mom and reevaluate the plan of care. It's enormously costly, but fortunately we can afford it, and it's money well spent. In a way, we're buying peace of mind, because if Mom were in a nursing home she'd be really unhappy, and that would make us all unhappy."

If you do have the money, if you are able to enlist the aid of a home-care agency, you will still want to know how to go about choosing the right agency. Personal recommendations—finding people you know who have had a good experience in utilizing the services of the agency—are always useful, as are referrals from doctors who know both you and your parent.

The National Association for Home Care (519 C Street N.E., Washington, DC 20002-5809; [202] 547-7424) publishes a brochure titled "How to Choose a Home Care Agency" that lists several considerations and covers such matters as accreditation, Medicare certification, and licensing, as well as costs and services. Among the questions to be asked by patients and their families:

- Does a nurse or therapist conduct an evaluation of your needs in the home? What is included: consultations with family members? with the patient's physician? with other health professionals?
- Does the agency send supervisors to visit your home regularly and evaluate the quality of care? Who do you call with questions or complaints?
- What plans or arrangements are made for you if your reimbursement sources are exhausted?

Medicaid-eligible patients are also provided with in-home services through an agency, although they have little say in selecting the company they deal with. Nonetheless, the same expectations for standards of care are in effect. Questions about such matters as consultation, supervision, and where to complain are also appropriate.

Other Ways to Locate an Aide

For people in the middle—those not rich enough to afford home-care fees set by private agencies or poor enough to qualify for Medicaid entitlements—some creativity is called for in finding kindly and qualified people to care for your parent at home. But it can be done.

Informal sources: Caregiver Laura Wolensky (see also chapter 6) was able to work out an arrangement with her parents' next-door neighbor, who agreed to provide the older couple with care until they moved to a nursing home. Especially in small-town communities, neighbors may be willing to pitch in with care, to provide meals, to drive the older person to the doctor, to check in and make sure that he or she is all right.

Sometimes people hear about good caregivers through word of mouth. In our own family, a neighbor's recommendation brought us together with the woman who now tends to my mother-in-law. We are daily grateful for the quality of care provided by this gentle, compassionate woman. But there were others before her who were not as competent. The first attendant you hire may not be the one who works out. Informal arrangements work best when family caregivers are available and involved in a parent's care, providing supervision and support and filling in on those days when the paid caregiver is ill or otherwise fails to show up.

Other family caregivers have located home-care providers through local churches and community centers, as well as caregiver support groups.

Working with the Home-Care Attendant

In choosing an aide, it is helpful to look for someone whose work experience includes elder care and, even better, someone who knows how to manage your parent's disability: to prepare the right kind of diet for a diabetic, for example, or deal with the erratic behavior of a dementia sufferer. Keep in mind, however, that experience is a guide, but not a guarantee. Just because the aide worked well with one patient does not mean that she will work well with *your* patient, who may be at a different stage of the illness, or whose personality may clash with the temperament of the aide. In interviewing aides, be clear about the patient's difficulties and foibles. See if they're willing to accept the challenge.

Look for maturity—a quality, not an age. You want someone in charge who is able to take responsibility but who is confident enough to involve the family when necessary.

Flexibility is also an important asset. As the condition of the patient changes, so will the demands on the home-care attendant. (A change in my mother's schedule required her home-care assistant to arrive earlier two mornings a week, for example, which she agreed to do.) Is the person you hire willing to alter her schedule or take on new and different tasks, within reason?

You also want someone who will not be condescending to the frail elder, but will treat your parent with respect (including calling her Mrs. Smith instead of Annie, if that is the way your parent would most comfortably be addressed). Adult children can be very helpful in encouraging respect by sharing information about the parent with the aide—what the parent's background was, his or her childhood, adulthood, occupation, and hobbies . . . including anecdotal material.

On the subject of nursing aides and the frail older persons whom they care for, I remember somewhere reading the following: *You think of the person who* was; *they deal with the person who* is. It is important for adult children to introduce the aides—through snapshots and stories—to the whole human being who now needs to be cared for.

It's important, as well, to treat the home-care aide with the respect she deserves. When you visit your parent, take some time to talk with the attendant. Ask about her background, her family, her likes and dislikes. Bring a treat that she will enjoy, something that shows you've thought of her and that you care.

After you hire a competent person, don't be on his or her back. A check-in phone call both morning and evening is not excessive; phoning the caregiver every hour on the hour is. It may be hard for the adult child to cede authority to others, but it is helpful (to all concerned) to do so. It also helps to let the aide know where you can be reached, if and when necessary.

Finally, try not to involve the aide in family issues that sometimes crop up in caregiving: the fact that you're experiencing tension with a spouse; the disappointment or anger you may feel toward a sibling. Your goal is to support the home-care aide and keep her attention centered on the patient. Ultimately, that is what helps the caregiver most.

CHAPTER 3

STRESS AMONG SIBLINGS— WAYS TO MANAGE IT

⸎

Reports by caregivers indicated . . . that siblings were overwhelmingly the most important source of interpersonal stress.

—FROM A STUDY BY SOCIOLOGISTS J. JILL SUITOR OF LOUISIANA STATE UNIVERSITY AND KARL PILLEMER OF CORNELL UNIVERSITY

When children become involved in caring for their aging parents, the family dynamic is altered in many ways. Sibling relationships change—not necessarily for the better, as studies show.

Inequitable Assignment of Responsibility Is a Source of Stress

According to Dr. Lenise Dolen, vice president of the National Association of Professional Geriatric Care Managers, "In 99.9 percent of cases, one of the siblings takes on most of the responsibility for the parent's care, is the decision maker or major caregiver, and the others are usually very content to let that happen."

The responsible sibling is less satisfied with this arrangement. Instead of finding her load eased by the family rallying round, this primary caregiver (most often, a woman) experiences added tension caused by unmet expectations of sibling cooperation and support. Negative feelings crop up even among brothers and sisters who were getting along fine before the demands of their parent's illness turned them into adversaries.

Acknowledging those feelings, and finding ways to place them in perspective, can be useful in reducing caregiver stress, as is illustrated by the following account told to me by a sixty-one-year-old woman.

Alma Oldham, vice president of personnel at a midsized corporation, has spent over a decade struggling to manage her job, her family, and the care of a mother and father who were both ailing. Suffering from emphysema, Alma's father has been in and out of hospitals. In the early stages of her father's illness, Alma saw her main task as being supportive of her mother, who was then the major caregiver. Both Alma and her brother, Ethan, would visit their parents' home, although Ethan did do so less frequently. *He has a wife and young children,* Alma would tell herself, making excuses for her younger brother, whom she loved dearly. Her tolerance was tested, however, after their mother suffered a series of strokes and Ethan virtually removed himself from the scene.

Alma recounts, "The strokes left our mother confused, combative, and utterly incapable of caring for my father. Further, these two older people, who had always been such devoted partners, began to take their misery out on one another. They would phone my home at all hours of the day or night, complaining about the awful things each of them said or did to the other. They needed a mediator. Shifts of hired help were required to tend to their physical needs. None of the aides stayed long. I would then find myself rushing from home to office to my parents' house or hospital (wherever they were to be found on any given day) to see how well they were managing, if they were receiving the right care, sometimes even whether they would make it through to the next morning. My husband complained. I developed an ulcer.

"At some point, I found myself bitterly resenting the fact that I was doing so much for my parents while my brother— who was also their child—was doing nothing. I had terrible feelings toward Ethan and I didn't know what to do about them. Then I sat myself down and said, 'I'm doing all of this for my parents because of my own need, my own sense of obligation. I'm doing what *I* need to do. Let Ethan decide what he needs to do, and if he chooses to do little else but visit our parents once in a while, so be it. But if I get so overloaded that I'm no longer able to manage their care, *that's* when I'll cry for help.'

"The time never came, but a curious thing happened after our mother died. Ethan was riddled with guilt. I felt no guilt, only sadness. I had done all that I could have done."

Negative thoughts aren't healthy. They drain the caregiver

of strength that is better used to tend to the needs of an aging parent . . . and to care for oneself. In clarifying the focus of her caregiving efforts, Alma was able to deal with her feelings toward her brother, set them aside, and move on. The brother-sister relationship remains strong today.

Hope, a primary caregiver to two aged parents, speaks about her brother, Selwin. In one breath, she calmly explains that Selwin lives abroad and is unable to take an active part in their parents' care. "I'm simply grateful that he doesn't countermand my decisions," she says. In the next breath, Hope tells me that she suspects that her brother moved abroad because he wanted to place some distance between himself and the family. "He knew that I'd do whatever was needed whenever it became necessary," she says. "I have always been the responsible one. He is the wanderer." Her voice has an edge to it now. "Thank God for my friends, especially those who are also coping with ailing parents. They're the ones I turn to for comfort and support."

Dad's Pet, Mom's Favorite, and Other Issues That Come into Play

Of course, the matter of strained relationships between brothers and sisters involves a lot more than the question of gender roles. So many other considerations can come into play, including the ages of the siblings, their own family situations (whether they are single, married, divorced, have child-care responsibilities), geographic distance, financial abilities, economic complexities (whether a business or inheritance is part of the family picture), the relationship of the siblings to their parents and to one another prior to the onset of the parents' illness. . . . For each family, each sibling group, the specifics are different. Yet there is much that seems, amazingly, the same.

When adult children become involved in caring for their parents, it is not unusual for them to regress to an earlier stage of life in their sibling relationships, to find themselves reenacting childhood scripts, keeping tally on who's doing more chores, who's receiving more privileges. Childhood rivalries resurface, old wounds are reopened, and, like Carol Waigner, whom we meet next, we may find that they still smart.

As she moves into a caregiving role, Carol—wife, mother, and accomplished artist—is upset by the fact that her two older brothers are (still) being allowed more freedom than she. Carol does not look her forty-six years. She tends to dress in jeans and loose sweaters, wears her shoulder-length hair in bangs, and speaks in a little-girl voice that belies her strength and achievements. She describes the family in which she grew up:

"My parents had two sons before I came along. My brother Jonathan is five years older than I am, and Robert is ten years my senior. I was the baby, and the girl, and my mom was ecstatic. She always called me 'My child for my old age.' That put a heavy burden on me, one that I'm certainly struggling with now.

"Mom wanted the boys to be independent, but she gave me mixed messages. My brothers attended an Ivy League college, and my mother told me I would have the same opportunity, and I did. She then encouraged them to go out and see the world. She encouraged me to become a dutiful wife and daughter. The boys traveled to Europe after college, and I went to graduate school so that I could become an art teacher (a good profession for a woman, according to my mother). My brothers basically left me to grow up as an only child. They took jobs out of town and would visit infrequently. After college, I married a man whom I knew my mother would be pleased with. He found my friends too Bohemian, I found his too boring. I bolted from the marriage.

"Twelve years ago, at about the time that I married my present husband, my parents moved to Florida. They're both seventy-eight now, and my dad has really deteriorated. He has diabetes, a heart condition, and memory lapses. His weight has gone from 180 to 150 pounds. He's been hospitalized frequently.

"The last time that Dad was in the hospital, Robert, the prodigal son, didn't even phone. He's very self-absorbed, claiming that the demands of his work and family preclude him from being actively involved with our parents, but I don't think that's any excuse. On the rare occasions when Robert does show up, everyone makes a fuss. He hasn't been to see our mother and father in two years now.

"John phones our folks from time to time. My parents appointed John the executor of their estate. I know they were thinking that I'm not supposed to worry my pretty little head about serious matters. Yet I also know that when the time comes to settle my parents' affairs, all the work will fall to me. I'm the one who flies down to Florida when either my mother or father needs help. I'm also the one who worries about what will happen to Mom when Daddy dies. Yet once in a blue moon, when my mother recognizes my efforts, she'll say, 'Well, this is what girls do.' It gets me really angry . . . at her and at my brothers."

Carol has begun to see a therapist to deal with that anger. The therapist is helping her understand how and why much of today's resentment is based on yesterday's grievances. She is also encouraging Carol to define what she wants from her brothers and to be specific in her demands. And that is helpful. For example, when their father's medical problems worsened, Carol placed a conference call to her brothers and told them, "You each have a choice. Either we go down, see the folks together, and decide with them what we're going to do next, or I will make the trip alone and you two will be responsible for my plane fare."

The brothers paid for Carol's ticket, and everyone felt okay with the decision. Asking for the help you need, and being specific, is one of the guiding principles of successful caregiving.

The Far-Away Favorite

The warm reception accorded the prodigal son is another matter, however—one that Carol continues to find upsetting. It is a fairly common scenario: the son or daughter who provides the most care is taken for granted, while the one at a farther remove is favored. Gerontologist Amy Horowitz explains: "It's not unusual for generational conflicts to arise between a parent and the child who is taking primary responsibility for day-to-day care. It's hard for the older person to give up that responsibility." And so he is apt to lash out at the child on whom he is most dependent. "The one across the country then becomes the favored child."

That the situation is explainable doesn't mitigate its harmful effect on the health and welfare of the primary caregiver.

Nor does it take into account the emotions of the less-involved sibling—feelings of guilt, of unworthiness. "I am grateful to my sister for taking on the main responsibility for our mother's care, but she never ceases to remind me of that fact," says a Midwestern woman of her sister who lives on the East Coast, near their mother. "Also, she's so competent, I don't think she wants or needs any help. I think she'd really rather do it herself."

Adult children who feel that they are not getting the cooperation they would like from brothers or sisters would do well to ask themselves this question: Am I in any way responsible for my sibling taking a lesser role in our parents' care? Have I been reaching out for help or keeping my siblings at bay? There is no question that it is important for you, the caregiver, to reach out for the help that you need. It's also true that, in certain situations, this advice is easier given than taken.

Rose Dobrof, executive director of The Brookdale Center on Aging and professor of gerontology at Hunter College of the City of New York, explains why. "Just telling someone to 'Reach out to your siblings,' doesn't take into account the complexity of the relationship," she says. "*You hate to have to ask.* You expect, you wish, that your siblings would be responsive to your needs: for respite, for help, for solace, et cetera. If they don't offer, you say 'To heck with them' and you do it yourself. That kind of thing can snowball, so that the primary caregiver can begin to exclude other people.

"Caregivers would do well to look into what keeps them from getting the help they need: Why haven't you asked your brother for help? Is it because you think he should know to offer? Is it because you've never had the kind of relationship where you have felt you could deal honestly with one another? Is it because you really want to have it all to yourself—is this your chance to exclude your sibling from a relationship with your mother? Sometimes it is very helpful for people who are caught up in this kind of resentful thinking to bring their worst feelings to the light of day and know . . . they're really not so dangerous. It may then be possible to move on."

Shared Decision Making: Letting Siblings Have Their Say Is Helpful

Sonya is someone who has had to *learn* to ask for help. She and her sister, Miriam, live in the same city as their mother, Rose. Their brother, David, lives in a neighboring state. All through the years, it's been Sonya, the take-charge sister, who orchestrated most of the family's special events. Whenever a birthday, anniversary, or holiday came around, everyone would gather at Sonya's home. It was a large house, and Sonya was an able, gracious hostess.

When their father died, it was only natural for the family to assemble at Sonya's home to mourn. And when their mother became frail and forgetful, Sonya forged ahead, doing everything possible to enable the older woman's continued residence in her own apartment. She replaced area rugs with wall-to-wall carpeting, had safety bars installed in the bathroom, hired women to see to her mother's care. She was dismayed to learn that her efforts were not appreciated by her siblings. Nobody said thank you.

Brothers and sisters may have different ideas about how to deal with the problem of an aging parent. They may have different abilities and concerns. And different levels of tolerance. Such differences need to be respected.

"I thought we would all agree that staying in her own home was best for Mom," says Sonya, "but my sister, Miriam, did not see it that way. She believed that it was not good for our mother to be isolated in her apartment, that she needed to be around other people. She felt that Mom should be living in a nursing home geared to caring for patients with dementia. I was adamantly opposed to having Mom go to live in any sort of group residence. I accused Miriam of being indifferent; she accused me of being dogmatic. The difference in our points of view caused a lot of conflict between my sister and me. That was painful for us both.

"I had to realize that the issue wasn't just my mother, that my mother was part of a *family*, and that there were other people whose opinions and needs had to be considered. I then got in touch with my brother, David, and asked for his feelings on the matter. It turned out that he, too, favored a geriatric residence, and for many of the same reasons as Miriam. Plus, he said, he wasn't able or willing to use his vacation and any other spare time to help share the caregiving duties. 'It isn't possible for us all to be Mom's company keepers,' David said, 'and yet she needs people. It would be wonderful if we could find the right place.'

"He then offered to take some time off from work and help us look. I had never thought to ask him to do that. Reaching a shared decision took a lot of the burden off me. Eventually, we made arrangements for Mom to enter a congregate living facility. I visit her there several times a week."

Communication is critical to successful caregiving. According to Daniel Fish, president of the National Academy of Elder Law Attorneys, "The issue of sibling stress comes up in almost every case where there's more than one child. And the best situations are the ones in which the adult child who is the major caregiver is keeping everybody else informed.

"I have seen many situations where the one primary caregiver feels overburdened and doesn't keep everyone informed about what's going on with the parents," says the attorney. "The other children feel treated unfairly, feel they haven't been given all the information about choices in medical treatment, or about finances, and that certainly can lead to disagreement."

And if the siblings are uninvolved in a parent's care?

"Then it is even *more* important to keep them informed," says Fish. "When I see a situation where the out-of-town sibling tells the one who is on the scene, 'It's okay. You do what you think best about our parent,' that is exactly the situation when I tell the caregiving child, 'Be extra sure to let that distant sibling know what you're doing.' I'm concerned that later on the nonresident caregivers will feel that they were left out. Keeping your siblings informed can go a long way in avoiding the rancor and dissension within the family that is often a legacy of parental illness."

Confronting the Anger: Counseling and Conferences

Another fairly typical situation is described by a caregiver:

"Suppose that I live in the same city as my mother, who has a chronic illness. My siblings are scattered across the country. As a result, I'm the one who has to do everything for Mom. I take her to doctors, and monitor her treatment. I see that her refrigerator is well stocked. I prepare meals, and leave them for her. I run myself ragged to see to it that she's eating right, keeping clean, getting her hair cut. It's gotten to the point where I no longer have a life of my own. Everything, it seems, revolves around Mom's condition, her needs. She and I have some good days, and some that are very difficult. And then there are days when the relentlessness of the situation seems much more than I can bear.

"On just such a day, I'm likely to receive a phone call from one of my sisters and brothers. 'I spoke to Mom yesterday,' they'll tell me, sounding perky and pleased. 'She sounded fine. Really good.' And I start stewing inside. *Why, sure, she sounded fine,* I think, *because I see to it that all of her needs are met. Why don't you come out once in a while and see what's involved in taking care of our mother? Why don't you offer to relieve me, if only for a week or so?* I find myself feeling incredibly tense, and resentful, and I don't like the anger. It threatens to consume me. What can I do to help myself?"

I ask Dr. Robert Butler for his advice. "One thing for a caregiver in this situation to do is seek counseling," he says. "There are agencies, many of which have fine social workers who can help.

"Another thing is to arrange a family conference. In a calmer moment, write to your sister and brother and ask for a conference call. Send a thoughtful letter, laying out the circumstances: 'When you guys call, frequently Mom sounds pretty good. But here's the usual day.' Describe your day and what you have to confront. Then lay out an agenda: 'Here's what I would like us to talk about.'

"When the actual call takes place, there may be legal, financial, and personal aspects to the discussion," he continues. "Let's look at the legal considerations, for example. You say, 'Mom says she doesn't want to be kept alive under the following circumstances. We've spoken to the doctors . . .'

Then your sister from San Francisco chimes in and says, 'Do everything possible to keep Mom alive.' You reply, 'That's not what Mom wants, so let's be clear about what Mother really wants, so you won't feel that I'm trying to impose my decision' . . . or 'Mom has made a will. I don't know what she's got in the will, but just so there won't be any conflict in the future, just know that she's seen a lawyer.'

"Your second concern may be financial. 'I've had to miss a lot of work, and I've also put out a lot of money, getting Mom's medication, picking up food. I would appreciate it if you'd consider sharing this financial burden with me. I'd be happy to send you the bills for any given month to give you a sense of what this has meant, both in terms of probable loss of productivity for me, maybe its effects on my promotion or raises. I don't know how easily I can document that for you, but I can send you the other costs—transportation, hiring someone to substitute for me when I can't be at Mom's and she needs help. And I'd appreciate your sharing the costs. [Finances can become a very complex issue; see chapter 6 for a fuller discussion.]

" 'There is a personal side, as well, and I'd appreciate your understanding. If I seem irritable or tired when I speak with you, it's a consequence not of any personal negative feelings toward you guys, but there are moments when I wish to heck you were here doing all of this instead of me, because it really is tough; it's very hard to deal with. And another reason I want to talk to you and go through this agenda is not to make you feel guilty and not to create problems, but ultimately and hopefully to reduce the possibility that later on you will feel some discomfort because you will feel that you didn't share in caring for Mom. When can you make visits or have Mother visit you? Let's set up schedules for when your vacation is due, see if there's some chance of your taking a trip in this direction, because time is short, and if you feel that you would like to spend more time with our mother, you don't want to come to that decision after she's gone.'

"Of course," Butler adds, "that's just an idea of what can be said. You can't give anyone an exact script."

Family conferences can take place over the phone or in person. It may be useful to employ the services of a facilitator: a social worker at the hospital or clinic that your parent visits, a professional on the staff of the day-care center, a geriatric care manager, someone knowledgeable about the aging process and about family dynamics, someone able to direct the conversation in an unemotional manner.

At one point, not long after my own mother's condition was diagnosed, my sister, brother, and I benefited from such a family conference. It was moderated by a nurse, who answered questions about our mother's condition, and a social worker, who helped us to talk about feelings and establish some cooperative arrangements for parent care. All three siblings left the meeting feeling closer and better directed. With the passage of time, however, some of our finest resolutions went by the board. People fall into old habits of overinvolvement or distancing. The inequities may be unintentional, but they do cause ill feelings. I have been thinking, lately, about scheduling another family conference.

Over time, I have developed a personal list of rules for handling sibling relationships with minimum stress and maximum efficiency. I'd like to share them with you.

Number one, the cardinal rule of survival, is tacked up on my bulletin board: DON'T EXPECT ANYTHING.

"Don't expect" should not be misconstrued to suggest that it's somehow wrong to *ask* a brother, sister, or other relative for help. It does not mean "Don't make arrangements for others to share the load." If you are the primary caregiver and you cannot do it all, try to find other ways to manage (perhaps by arranging for weekend help or periodic respite care), but don't walk around filled with resentment over what your sibling is not doing. None of us can be responsible for someone else's decisions, or expect them to share our emotional commitment. Don't expect, and you won't be disappointed.

The corollary to that is equally important: DO MAKE SURE THAT YOUR SIBLINGS KNOW THAT YOU APPRECIATE THE GOOD THINGS THEY DO. Speak positively: "I'm glad you visited Mom the other day. How was she?" instead of "So you finally visited Mom the other day. It's about time." It is helpful for siblings to support one another in times of family stress, not tear each other down.

Number two: BE VERY CLEAR ABOUT WHAT YOU'RE ABLE TO DO AND WHAT YOU CANNOT DO. Whatever your level of commitment to your parent's care, let your siblings know what you're prepared to do, and accept their assessment of how much, and how, they're able to be involved.

Number three: BE OPEN AND HONEST. Don't try to manipulate the actions of your siblings by sending messages through a third party. If you think that your disabled parent should be included in your sister's birthday bash, say so, leaving room for your sister to explain why she thinks that may not be a wise idea, and providing the possibility of compromise—perhaps your parent can be brought to the party, but leave early. Don't ask the home-care attendant to ask your sister if she's going to invite your mother to the party. People know when they are being manipulated. It leads to strained feelings.

Number four: BE RESPONSIBLE. If you say you're going to do something, *do it*. For example, if you agree to visit your parent every third weekend, make the visit. Let your siblings know that they can count on you. Don't create a situation in which your participation must be negotiated on a weekly basis. That causes tension.

Number five: BE FORGIVING. When her mother came down with ALS (amyotrophic lateral sclerosis, commonly known as Lou Gehrig's disease, a chronic, degenerative disease that causes muscle weakness and atrophy), Jocelyn did just about everything for her mother while her sister, Nancy, did very little. In the beginning, Jocelyn would visit two days a week, taking the train from her home in New Hampshire to her mother's place in northern Connecticut. When her mom could no longer manage on her own, even with some help, Jocelyn arranged a move to her own home in New Hampshire, where she had set up a room with special hospital equipment. An attendant was hired to manage her mother's personal care. When speech deserted the older woman, she was able to communicate by means of computer, and when even that failed her, Jocelyn enlisted the aid of a nearby hospice, which sent people into the home and provided some much-needed respite for Jocelyn until her mother's final days. Sister Nancy, who lived in New Mexico, was helpful in researching resources (it was her idea to get the computer), but basically stayed out of the picture, which caused Jocelyn to feel a lot of anguish.

And now? "I am trying to put the past behind me," says

Jocelyn. "I realize that my sister and I have different tem-
peraments. Nancy can't go into a sickroom, while I'm able to
handle physical care. Also, Nancy has told me that, for her,
our mother died when she ceased to be the parent we both
knew. For me, my mother was alive until, holding her as she
succumbed to pneumonia, I felt her draw her last breath. So
I understand that Nancy and I are different, and I'm able to
live with that now. After all, she's my sister, and I love her."

Jocelyn has helped me focus on what is really important.

To summarize, these are some of the things that caregivers
have found useful in helping them deal with sibling-related
stress:

- clarifying the focus of their own caregiving efforts;
- asking for help when necessary, and being specific;
- learning to function without sibling assistance when
  that becomes problematic;
- keeping less-engaged siblings informed about the
  parent's disability, desires, and care plans;
- listening to the sibling's point of view;
- confronting their anger and not allowing an irritation to fester;
- arranging a family conference;
- seeking professional counseling;
- turning to friends when family fails to offer the support and comfort that can help a caregiver get
  through the difficult moments. As J. Jill Suitor and
  Karl Pillemer concluded from their study, encouraging caregivers to draw upon the resources of friends
  who have themselves served as caregivers could

avoid many of the negative feelings provoked by sibling relationships and could increase the likelihood that caregivers would be provided with adequate support.

When push comes to shove in caring for aging parents, however, most brothers and sisters admit that they are glad they have one another even if there *are* some discordant moments between them. As we will see in the next chapter, the only child often feels far more disadvantaged.

CHAPTER 4

GOING IT ALONE:
THE ONLY CHILD

The only child confronts the challenges of parent care unconstrained by sibling pressures but also unsupported by a sibling presence. The weight of responsibility, the bittersweet experience of providing care, are his or hers by exclusive contract. Geriatric care manager Nick Newcombe, who grew up as an "only," remarks, "What is the statement that parents often make about their only children? It's 'They entertain themselves.' Later, those same children have to care for their parents themselves, too. They can be overwhelmed very fast."

"Overwhelmed" is the word that Theresa Longo uses to describe herself in the caregiving role. For the past four years, ever since she brought her mother, Stella, from Jersey

City to live near her in Santa Fe, New Mexico, the fifty-one-year-old daughter has found herself at the older woman's beck and call—her constant companion, chauffeur, caterer, visiting nurse, and liaison to the outside world. And she's done it alone. "I'd give my right arm for a sister," she says. "I felt that way as a child, and now I feel that way again. It's funny how I've come full circle."

Like many an only child, Theresa grew up as the apple of her parents' eye. "My mother was thirty-five, my father in his forties when I was born, and they always let me know I was a gift, something special. We three were a unit, for better or worse. Dad was the strict parent, Mom the easygoing one. Together, it balanced out.

"Eight years ago, Dad died of a heart attack. Afterward, Mom would fly out to Boston, where we then lived, for family celebrations—her birthday, the birthdays of my son and daughter (her grandchildren), my daughter's wedding—and she would stay for two weeks. It was wonderful to have Mom with us and to know that, when she returned home to New Jersey, she'd be surrounded by family: two sisters, three brothers, and a bevy of nieces and nephews, everybody visiting back and forth.

"Mom has chronic lymphocytic lymphoma, leukemia-like tumors that need to be treated periodically. The condition has grown more invasive with the passage of time. Five years ago, shortly after my family moved to Santa Fe, we had Mom come and see a doctor out here. She had some mild chemotherapy, which she took fairly well, but I noted that she was a lot frailer than she had been. Mom could no longer reach us via a direct flight; she was required to change planes, which she found very difficult, and so I would have to fly east, pick her up and bring her here, then make the return trip in similar fashion.

"While I was in her home, I began to notice some confusion. She couldn't manage her bank statements. Furthermore, although she was surrounded by family, she didn't seem to interact with them very much. She'd just sit there and wouldn't participate in the conversation. That's when I began to think about finding a place for Mom in a retirement community nearer my home. I broached the subject to my mother, and she was amenable to it. It seemed like a good idea. She could be with our family more often, and I could take a more active role in her care when it became necessary."

Just how active that role would be, and how it would affect her own family life, was not something that Theresa anticipated. She says, "Since I went away to college, I had never lived in the same city as my parents, which gave me a different way of functioning. They were not a part of my everyday existence. We did not sit down to Sunday dinner together. When my mom came out here, I thought it would take her a while to adjust, but I didn't realize how much adjusting *I* would have to do.

"Once my mother was settled in her new home, I began to see her in a different light. I'd always thought of her as social and gregarious because I'd seen her in a setting where she was surrounded by a large and loving extended family. People were always popping in and out of one another's homes. Suddenly, I became aware that my mother was basically not a very social person.

"She did not reach out to the other residents of the retirement home, but expected to be part of *my* everyday existence. She has made me very much aware that I am her only connection in Santa Fe. I used to see Mom every day, bring her home with me every other day. My husband, Pete, did not enjoy having my mother around. He found it depressing. I felt like I was in the middle. It caused a lot of friction between us."

Theresa found herself constantly tired and edgy. A woman who seldom topped the scales at over 117 pounds, she began to lose weight—a result of stress, said a doctor she consulted. It was clear that she needed to make some changes, and soon.

Marital Conflict as a Contributor to Caregiver Stress

Research indicates that having an adult child take on the caregiver role can be just as dramatic a transition for a family as, for example, having a wife and mother return to work. In each case, time and attention are diverted from the nuclear family unit. Children may resent not having Mommy readily available to them. Spouses, in particular, can place added pressure on a caregiving partner who's already on overload.

In a study titled "Family Caregiving and Marital Satisfaction," sociologists J. Jill Suitor and Karl Pillemer found that "husbands' dissatisfaction with their wives' performance of family roles generally focused on the way in which caregiving directly affected the men's own lives rather than changes in other aspects of family life. In part the focus on the husbands' own needs . . . may have been because most of the couples did not have young children at home."

Husbands' dissatisfaction, the researchers found, "generally focuses on the ways in which the women's new responsibilities reduce their time for social activities or intimacy, or necessitate an increase in the husband's contribution to household labor."

It should be noted, however, that dissatisfaction with a spouse's commitment to caregiving is not the exclusive reaction of husbands. When the only child is a man who becomes the primary caregiver to an ailing parent, as was true for Stephan Moore, whom we met in chapter 1, we often also find spousal disagreement around the subject of parent care. This can be particularly distressing to the only child who, because he or she does not have any siblings to turn to, must instead rely heavily on the support provided by spouse and children. When tensions arise over caregiving issues, the only child is apt to feel them most keenly.

The first big step Theresa took toward helping herself was to address the marital friction. "I just said to Pete, 'Look, I will try my best to give us as much private time as possible, but to a certain extent I really do have to look after my mother. I'm an only child, and that's the way it is.' Pete had undergone a coronary not too long before my mother moved near us, and I think that he was suffering the mild depression that frequently follows cardiac surgery. I think that at that time he would have appreciated being the center of my attention. The situation has eased up a lot as he's felt better.

"When Pete is out of town," Theresa says, "I use the time to have Mom stay with me, so that maybe I can spend less time with her when he is here. That's one of the tricks of the trade that I've developed. The next step in my commitment to making time for the couple relationship was to establish Saturdays as a time for Pete and me to spend together—exclusively.

"Mom always has Friday and Sunday dinners with us, and

stays over on Sunday nights, but I invent a story, each week, about why she and I can't be together on Saturday. I say that Pete and I have to meet with one of his business partners or that we have a dinner to attend. I'm afraid I have found that 'inventing' has become a really useful tactic. It's so much easier to make up a story than to tell my mother I just want to spend Saturdays with my husband, because that offends her. Nobody enjoys making up stories, but I have to . . . and it works."

Theresa and Pete's children have also pitched in. Although their daughter is married and their son is away at college, each has been called into service for a week at a time, enabling their parents to take a well-earned vacation. Says Theresa, "When our son is at home, or when anyone else is around who knows my mother well enough so that I don't have to explain her to them, it is much easier for me than when it's just my mother and me. Whenever I can increase the field by one other person who belongs, the pressure on me is greatly lessened."

Volunteerism serves as another saving grace. A relative newcomer to the community *and* an only child, Theresa recognized that she needed to develop a support system, and volunteered at the local medical center, where she spends every Wednesday as a patient advocate. "That day keeps me sane," she says, adding, "but the absolute highlight of my week is my involvement in a local charity that helps battered wives.

"When the idea of my joining the organization first came up," she says, "I remember thinking, *My gosh, how am I going to do that with all that I have to do with my mother?* In point of fact, this connection has probably been the single biggest help I have found. Some people hate meetings, but if

I respect the cause and I like the people involved, I find the interaction and social contact rewarding.

"When you're dealing one-on-one with a parent who is ill or a parent who is somewhat demented, you need the kind of social contact that teaches you that the world is stimulating and interesting. So, since I know that this helps me, I will very often arrange to see my mother following a meeting or luncheon, knowing that the energy from the meeting will carry me through the afternoon.

"I've gained back five pounds, so I guess I'm handling the situation much better now."

Caregiving When Communication with a Parent Isn't Easy

Where Theresa has learned to take a few steps back in caring for her mother, Georgina Frost Adams is trying to discover how best to step in . . . how to care for a father who insists that he's all right despite signs that say otherwise, how to respect a parent's independence and privacy and nonetheless manage to do the right thing.

Georgina is fifty-six, married, the mother of two children, and lives in Charleston, South Carolina. Her father, William, a widower, is eighty-four, but most people take him for many years younger. He carries himself as a man who has always been handsome, and still rises early to get to the office—a rented room in which he does his writing. "It's more a matter of pride than productivity nowadays," says his daughter, although he has the Emmys, now dusty, to show for a successful television writing career.

It is that same pride, Georgina thinks, that has kept her

father from fessing up to his declining health and memory lapses. "He's a real Southern-gentleman type," she says. "A lot of stuff is not said. I think he's created a persona for himself of this good-looking, vigorous older man who is still a player. That's both good and bad.

"Daddy had a car wreck a month ago," she explains. "He ran into two other people and he almost killed himself. Since he lives out in the country, far from any form of public transportation, I looked into ways that would make it possible for him to manage without a car. I found out which stores would deliver, gave him the names of transportation services, and even located a student who would drive my father on errands for a small fee. Daddy said, 'Thank you so much,' and then went out and bought a new car. That's pretty typical of our relationship. I do the research and make suggestions. He does what he wants."

It is a touchy situation. In general, however, gerontologists believe that it's important to respect the wishes of the older person. We cannot take over for our parents, just as we cannot run the lives of our own older children. What we can do is advise, support, and stand ready to help if and when our help is requested or needed.

Georgina says, "What bothers me, in addition to the safety factor, is that my father actually has some health problems, is quite lonely, and doesn't know how to ask for help or get it. For example, he has diabetes, but the way I found that out was when he had left some literature around his house one summer, two years ago. He left it in some very obvious places. I guess that I should have said something when I came upon the pamphlets, but I felt that it was his place to bring it up." Reticence has clearly been passed down in this family from one generation to the next.

Georgina continues, "The next thing I noticed was that Daddy was taking medication, but I never knew what for. His speech became slower; he had a thing where he was chewing on his cheek all the time. I was becoming frightened, and decided that I had to do something about it."

In her quest for information on her father's condition, Georgina phoned his doctor, who refused to tell her anything. ("If your daddy's got any worries about his health, let him come in and see me himself," he told the worried daughter curtly.) Georgina then visited her father's home, copied down the names of his various medications, and brought the list to a local pharmacist. "He said that the medications Daddy was taking could interact with one another, and that my description of Daddy's symptoms fit the profile of a particular medication. So I felt that I was on the right track, but how was I going to do anything with this information? That was my next problem."

Georgina phoned a nearby medical center and arranged an appointment with a gerontologist who guided her on how to talk with her father about difficult issues, like the following: "One incident that made me terrified had to do with Daddy's being visited by a young couple—let's call them the Brewsters—of whom he is very fond. A week later, he said to me, 'Have the Brewsters been here?' It wasn't 'Where are my keys?' This was a big deal. So the doctor explained to me, 'Instead of being impatient with your father, instead of saying *Of course they were here; don't you remember?*, just say, *They were here last weekend.* He told me to just give the answer without any criticism or impatience, not to fill in the synapses. I have found that helpful.

"With regard to my medical concerns, the doctor also suggested that I go back to my father's physician and work through him as much as possible, because my father would respect his doctor's authority. He advised me to tell the doctor that, as a family, we had noticed certain conditions, and that I had been selected as the point person for the family. Making it sound like I was representing Daddy's friends and family at large gave me more clout. Suddenly, I wasn't an only child; I was a community, and I didn't feel quite so helpless. The doctor had Daddy come in for a checkup. His medication was adjusted."

Surrounding a Parent with Life Helps the Adult Child as Well

Still, there was the question of her father's isolation to be dealt with. Although programs for seniors are available in the area, Georgina's father absolutely refuses to set foot in one. ("That's for old folks," he says.) His daughter expresses some frustration with this stance, and sees no parallel between the older man's position and the fact that there are support groups for adult children in the area, too, which *she* will not check out. (She says, "Some people like to sit in a room with ten or twelve people, but I don't. When I have a problem, the first people I turn to are some women friends who are going through the same thing. There's one friend in particular— we're like sisters; we have our ups and downs, but I know she is there for me.")

Georgina has been able to do something about her father's isolation. "There is a little cottage behind his house," she explains. "The tenant was an older gentleman who paid the rent on time but didn't really add to Daddy's quality of life. When this man left, I searched for and found a really nice young couple to live there. The husband does some chores around the house. The wife is a graduate student who comes by with home-baked brownies. There's also a room in the house that I'm encouraging my father to rent to a student. I think that if I can get him involved with people in this way, he won't be so isolated. This will make him feel better and it makes me feel better because I'm not carrying the burden of his loneliness.

"If you're an only child, as I am, the best way I know of to help yourself is to find people who can join your team in some way. Whether it's a family member or somebody outside, the way to survive is to reach out."

To sum up, here is what helped the only children manage their caregiving role:

- enlisting the cooperation of spouses and children;
- being clear about priorities;
- seeking out medical specialists (including pharmacists) for information and guidance;
- locating an appropriate geriatric residence;
- establishing partnerships to address a parent's solitude;
- finding new ways to communicate with the parent;
- volunteering, engaging in stimulating outside activities;
- turning to friends as family.

It's also helpful to keep in mind the wide range of programs and support available in the community (from friendly visitors to visiting nurses, day-care activities to respite programs). A phone call to your local Area Agency on Aging is the first step in reaching a network of people and programs that can help you and your aging parent. No caregiver needs to be alone.

And being far away from your parent need not prevent your being an effective, involved caregiver. The chapter that follows, on long-distance caregiving, discusses ways to do just that.

CHAPTER 5

LONG-DISTANCE
CAREGIVING

Mimi Davidson is about to turn sixty—a fact, she says, "that really bothers me because it puts me at the age where my parents were when I began to look at them as old." Her husband and children are planning a surprise party for her. Mimi could use a party right now. She could use *something* to relieve the stress, the ever-present anxiety caused by the situation that she finds herself in at this stage of her life. An only child, Mimi is solely responsible for managing the care of her parents—her father, ninety-one, and mother, eighty-eight—who make their home in Florida, where they've lived for the past seventeen years. Mimi and her husband, Ted, live in Westport, Connecticut. Their children are grown and no longer live at home.

Mimi's father is hard of hearing, and won't wear a hearing aid. "Did you get my check, Daddy?" she asks him. He answers, "What do you need a truck for?" Aggressive treatments for prostate cancer have left her father incontinent and enfeebled. He wears a condom catheter—a bag attached to his leg that has to be drained. Mimi's mother has become very forgetful. "I thought it was bad when I had to write everything down for her on a calendar," Mimi says. "Nowadays my mother doesn't know where the calendar *is*.

"People tell me, 'Your parents have each other.' The way I see it, my parents have problems. Yet here I am in Connecticut, and I have to surmise what's going on with my parents in Florida. 'How are you?' I ask when I phone them. They answer, 'We're getting along as well as we can.' To see your parents failing is devastating. But I'm up here, and I don't see it regularly. That's good and that's bad. I've hired a next-door neighbor to see to their care. She tells me, 'Sometime in the near future you've got to make other plans.' Does that mean placing them in a home? If so, should I investigate places in Florida where it's warm or in Connecticut, to have them near me? Where do I turn? What do I do next?

"My parents may not be living with me. I may not be getting up in the middle of the night for them, but they are driving my life. Let me tell you, this business of being a long-distance caregiver is very, very tough."

Tough, but far from unique. Ours is a society on the move, one in which it has become fairly common for grown children to leave home to pursue different lifestyles and work opportunities. Nor do our parents necessarily stay put. During the past decade, the number of people sixty-five and older who moved from one state to another, as did Mimi's parents, increased by 65 percent. As a result of all this mobility, a growing number of today's adult sons and daughters are discovering just how hard it is to try to ensure the welfare of aging parents who live hundreds, sometimes thousands, of miles away. Long-distance caregiving is sometimes referred to as "passive caregiving." That's not necessarily so.

Susan Eberle, fifty-seven, is an active caregiver who, slowly and steadily, is succeeding in managing the complex demands of meeting her mother's needs and her own as well. Susan, who is single, lives in New York; her brother Daniel, fifty-five, lives with his wife and two children in California; a second brother, James, fifty-three, married and with one child, resides in Washington, about an hour's drive from the Maryland home of their mother, Annette, eighty-nine. Susan has mixed feelings toward her mother. "She's a very crotchety and cranky old lady," the daughter will tell you in one breath. And in another: "She is strong, she is honorable. I love her."

From the age of seventy-five, Annette Eberle suffered a number of health problems, undergoing a gallbladder operation and surgery for two hip replacements. Although she recovered well each time, the hospitalizations and follow-up care ate into her savings, which were meager at best. Susan worried constantly about her mother, who lived alone. The daughter would place a call to her mother's home every evening at six to check on her welfare. Every third Saturday, Susan boarded an Amtrak train to Maryland, where she would spend the weekend with her mother, returning to the city and her job on Monday morning.

"The first twenty-four hours of each of these visits would be spent letting my mother rave about her gripes in life—her health, her poverty, her failed marriage," says Susan. "By Sunday, Mom was in a better mood. We'd go to church, have lunch, and watch television." One Sunday, Susan heard about an elderly church member who had fallen, broken her hip, and lain on the floor dehydrating for three days until somebody found her. "That was a turning point for me," she says. "From then on, I lived in constant fear that something like that would happen to my own mother, and I knew I would have to do something about it."

Considering a Move

A quick-fix solution to this problem of distant caregiving might seem to be to have the parents relocate, to bring them nearer the grown children and their families, perhaps even to create a new multigenerational household. Experts caution the older parent and the caregiving child against making such decisions without giving a good deal of thought to the consequences. As previously noted, a move away from familiar people, places, and things can be traumatic for the older person. Further, unless there is sufficient help available, having a parent come to live with the caregiver can be completely disruptive to life's everyday routines and rhythms. The caregiver has to ask herself not just *How will my parent get along?* but also *How will I manage?*

There have been moments, over the years, when Susan Eberle came very close to inviting her mother, Annette, to live with her, times when the daughter would find herself looking about her compact apartment and thinking, *If I made room for Mom in the alcove . . . If I bought a sofa bed . . .* But she quickly came face to face with three major realities. "Reality number one is that I live in a studio apartment, and can't afford a bigger place," she says. "Reality number two is that my job, in television sales, is very demanding. I work long hours and am frequently on the road. And I need my job. Reality number three is that there is a man in my life. So, no, I couldn't go to live with my mother, and I couldn't bring my mother to live with me.

"Then my mom became really frail, and began to lose it mentally," Susan continues. "During one visit, I saw my mother use a towel instead of a pot holder, and set the towel on fire. A CAT scan [a computerized image] of my mother's brain showed that she'd suffered some organic deterioration. So now, I also began to worry that she would burn her place down *if* she didn't waste away first. My mom was losing weight. She wasn't eating properly. I knew that something had to be done about that."

Scheduling Visits . . . and Making Them Count

Few long-distance caregivers are able to spend time with a frail, elderly parent as frequently or regularly as Susan. Work, family, and financial obligations, as well as emotional considerations, may preclude frequent trips. Notwithstanding these realities, the importance of paying visits to an aged or ailing parent cannot be stressed too strongly. The less frequently such visits take place, the more extended they ought to be. Visits should be used by the long-distance caregiver to reconnect with a parent, to provide respite for the primary caregiver, to reassess the situation. Is there sufficient food in the refrigerator? Is it fresh or moldy? Are medications being taken? Is the parent still able to drive? Is he or she getting out, and is anyone stopping by?

Knowing how well an older person is managing his or her life can be difficult if you live at a distance. During her daily phone calls, for example, Susan would never fail to ask her mother what she had eaten for dinner. "Don't worry," her mother would tell her, "I ate." Or "I had some soup." Or "I fixed myself a snack." When she visited her mother, Susan made it a habit to check the contents of the refrigerator and cupboard and was dismayed by what she found—more precisely, by what she *didn't* find. "My mother ate practically nothing," she says, "which had me very concerned. Then I hit upon the idea of buying her a high-protein, nutritional drink that is sold in drugstores. I would buy it by the caseload. She pretty much lived on that until I found out about a program that would deliver a hot, prepared lunch on weekdays. That was a great relief."

About Meals on Wheels and Other Nutritional Resources

Adequate nutrition is a major concern for the frail elderly. Many older people find it difficult to shop for and prepare their own meals. Further, the sense of taste may be weaker, leading to a diminished interest in food. Memory, too, plays a part in the decline. Many a time, for example, when I phone and ask my mother if she's had lunch or dinner, she will answer, "I don't remember." There are periods, it seems to me, when she must subsist entirely on orange juice and English muffins.

When my sister, brother, or I visit, we make certain to take Mom out to lunch and dinner. I will often stock Mom's refrigerator with packages of ready-made food, as well: chicken, cooked vegetables, salad, soup, but they last only so long. The doctor tells me that Mom needs albumin in her diet, that she ought to be eating more chicken, fish, and egg whites. I jot down his instructions, then take Mom out to lunch and order tuna fish.

But what about the rest of the time, *most* of the time, when my mother and I do not sit down to a meal together? She's provided with a hot lunch at the adult day-care program she attends twice weekly, and sometimes enjoys a congregate meal at a nearby senior center. Knowing that, I do not feel quite as guilty about not taking a more active role in her overall nutrition. But I don't feel fully reassured, either.

Responding to the problem of poor nutrition among the elderly, the Older Americans Act of 1965 established two major food programs:

- "Congregate meals" (generally, lunches) for anyone over sixty are available at most senior centers, five or seven days a week;
- For shut-ins, Meals on Wheels programs, found in many communities, will deliver food at low or no cost. Many religious and community organizations also provide food to needy older people.

To locate these programs, contact your Area Office on Aging, senior center, or religious organization. Since the demand often exceeds the supply, it's a good idea to learn about the programs, find out how to apply, and have your parent's name placed on a waiting list as soon as possible.

In addition to providing a nutritious lunch, Meals on Wheels serves a social function. The volunteer who delivers the meals may be the only one to visit the older person on any given day. This is especially helpful when sons or daughters live at a distance and are unable to check in on the frail elderly parent in person.

Investigate the Local Support Network

It's important for the long-distance caregiver to take a look at whatever informal support network exists in the parent's community and to find a trusted observer—a neighbor, minister, friend, or relative—who agrees to look in on the parent, perhaps to run errands or even to provide more intensive care. When you live at a distance, there needs to be some person at the other end whom you feel comfortable phoning or who will agree to call you collect when problems arise.

It's sometimes difficult for the long-distance caregiver to perceive the seriousness of a situation or to decide whether a parent's call for help is simply a wish for more frequent visits or a cry of distress requiring an immediate dash to the airport. For the long-distance caregiver, therefore, it is vitally important to identify some person you can trust at the other end of the line. "The nursing home sends home-care workers to care for my mother," says Nate, a long-distance caregiver, "but they come and go. In our case, there's a cleaning woman who has been with Mother for years. She looks in on Mother and does the grocery shopping. I send her a check, she cashes it, and she sees that my mother has money. She's someone Mother trusts, and I do, too."

For Susan Eberle and her mother, Annette, the angel of

mercy is a longtime younger friend of her mother's named Thelma Brown. "Thelma does the grocery shopping for Mom, takes her to the doctor, manages her checkbook," says Susan. "I have arranged for her to share power of attorney with me so that she can do the banking. If not for Thelma, I would have had to place my mother in the county home. More than anyone or anything, she's what helps me survive."

Thelma has refused to accept any compensation from Susan. Other caregivers have been able to work out financial arrangements with neighbors, building superintendents, or local students who agree to run errands or perform various chores to help the older parent manage his or her life.

Long-Distance Rates: Finances Are Often an Issue

It's not possible to take advantage of Frequent Flyer mileage or special reduced rates for advance booking when a flight must be arranged, and tickets bought, at a moment's notice. Telephone and travel expenses can mount quickly for the long-distance caregiver. In the Eberle family, money worries added to the tensions of parent care and created some problems among the siblings. Susan and James had all they could do to cover the monthly rent on their mother's apartment. They understood that Daniel was having a tough time making ends meet, but still they felt that he might have made a small contribution to their mother's care.

When the mail brought a letter from Annette Eberle's landlord announcing a large increase in rent, Susan was devastated. She determined that she had no choice but to appeal the decision. That meant having to bare the family's financial situation, to go public about something that had long been held private. Susan wrote and rewrote the letter she sent. "It basically said: 'This is my mother's situation. She has lived here for thirty years. She has limited income. Please do not impose this raise because my mother cannot afford it.'" The landlord replied, "Please send me copies of your mother's and your tax records. If what you say is verified, not only will I not increase your mother's rent but I will decrease it by a hundred dollars a month."

"And he did!" says Susan, elated by the deed and the memory of it. "That victory took a huge load off me. It also inspired me to become more aggressive in finding other ways that would help my mother and relieve some of the weight that my brother James and I had been carrying. The burden became even greater when my mother collapsed against the sofa on her eighty-seventh birthday, was rushed to the hospital, and underwent a double-bypass heart operation. James helped a lot. He would visit Mom daily in the hospital, and call in to me to report on her condition. I took three weeks off from my job so I could care for Mom when she came home."

The Family Leave Bill, passed by Congress in 1993, allows eligible employees up to twelve weeks per year of unpaid leave to care for a child or an aging relative. As a practical matter, however, many caregivers (like Susan) cannot afford to be away from their jobs or do without their weekly salary for that long. Susan knew that her mother would require the services of a home-care worker when the three weeks were up, and set about contacting several of the agencies listed in the telephone directory. The hourly rates that they quoted were far too high for Susan's budget.

In desperation, she visited the local Office on Aging—a logical *first* stop for caregivers who want to determine what services there are in the community for elders in need of assistance. They recommended an agency with reasonable rates. Says Susan, "I returned to them several times thereafter, as needed."

Telephone Assurance Programs

At church one Sunday, speaking with the minister's wife, Susan learned about a telephone assurance program staffed by volunteers who place daily calls to frail and disabled persons living alone. (Of interest is the fact that the volunteers are themselves residents of a senior facility.) If the person who is called doesn't answer at the designated check-in time, the volunteer then places a call to an emergency number provided by the family. Susan had her mother listed with the service, at no cost.

"The telephone service reassured me psychologically," she says. "Someone from the program would phone my mother in the morning, and I would place a call in the evening . . . because the thought is always in your mind: *She could be on the floor and in agony.* I no longer phoned Mom on weekends, however, which was extremely freeing. If I didn't hear from the service, I knew everything was all right."

Many organizations also participate in friendly visitor programs that provide regular visits to elders who aren't able to get out much. It is possible to link a homebound parent with someone whose interests are similar. For some time, for example, my mother-in-law enjoyed Scrabble games with a lovely middle-aged volunteer who would visit her on Wednesdays. These visits became a highlight of my mother-in-law's week.

The Geriatric Care Manager—When You Can't Be There Yourself

Susan also made an appointment to see a geriatric care manager, a professional (generally a licensed social worker, psychologist, or nurse) who specializes in assisting older people and their families with long-term care arrangements. Geriatric care managers perform a variety of services, including:

- assessing the parents' needs and the family's situation, identifying problems, eligibility for assistance, and need for services;
- arranging for in-home care, screening job applicants, and monitoring their performance;
- reviewing financial, legal, or medical issues and offering referrals to geriatric specialists;
- providing crisis intervention;
- acting as a liaison to faraway caregivers, and alerting families to problems;
- assisting with a move to or from a retirement complex, care home, or nursing home;
- offering counseling or support.

Thanks to geriatric care managers, sons and daughters living far from their parents (and nieces and nephews involved with the care of uncles and aunts who live at a distance) are able to have some peace of mind, knowing that the older person's needs are being met. Such services do not come cheap, however. Fees for an initial assessment can be over $200, and hourly rates for supervision and care run from $50 to $150 an hour, depending on the area of the country. There are also fees for housekeeping, companions, nurses, and for the filing of forms.

Susan paid $80 for a onetime, one-hour consultation with a geriatric care manager. She felt that it was money and time well spent. "The woman knew about community residences where my mother might have been able to live. I told her of my concern about emergencies, that I didn't know anyone to call upon if a phone call to my mother went unanswered: who would go over to the house and find out if everything was all right? She supplied me with names of some agencies, one of which was willing to do that. She also knew about lawyers, about obtaining a power of attorney. And she knew how to deal with a cantankerous older person, someone like my mother.

"I had been struggling with the problem of *how to say no* to some of my mother's requests without sounding like a rebellious child. What the care manager said was, when your parent asks for something outrageous or makes demands that you can't fulfill, just say 'I'm sorry, I can't do that.' No excuses. No explanations. I realized how that simple statement would cut off a long wrangle with my mother. It's a good thing to have that specific phrase, *I can't do that,* in your arsenal. That alone was worth the cost of a onetime visit."

My own introduction to the work of a geriatric care manager came about in the following manner. I was awakened one morning by a phone call from Arlington, Virginia. My good friends Marsha and Henry were both on the line. "We need help," said Marsha. "I think my aunt's in trouble," said Henry, his words stepping on those of his wife.

The problem, Henry explained, involved his aunt Mae, an ailing widow who had always treated Henry as the child she'd never had. Henry reciprocated her affection, and so he'd had no hesitation, when time and circumstances warranted his involvement, about accepting responsibility for seeing to Aunt Mae's care. But Mae—"a woman who has always known her own mind"—refused to leave her home in suburban New York and Henry and Marsha, both government workers, were not about to leave their jobs in Washington, D.C. So they did the next best thing: they respected Mae's wishes, hired a live-in housekeeper to help with her daily needs, and either visited Aunt Mae or had her stay with them from time to time.

They had, in fact, just returned from a visit to their aunt— and that was the reason for the call. "We're really troubled by what we saw," said Henry. "Aunt Mae didn't seem at all alert. She's always been a feisty woman, yet she appeared to be quite fearful. We also noticed some bruises on her arms and face, which her housekeeper ascribed to frequent falls. The bottom line is, we're not so sure that's the reason.

"We couldn't stay around to check out our suspicions," continued Henry, "but we need to have *someone* step in and let us know what's going on. We wondered if you knew of some professional, some organization in your area, that could help us out."

I gave my friends the number of a geriatric social worker, someone whose professionalism and compassion I respected. The counselor, whom they hired, paid several visits to Aunt Mae, deciding quickly that the older woman was a victim of abuse by her housekeeper. Swiftly he took over, firing the housekeeper and placing a trusted attendant in the home while he set about finding a residential placement for the older woman, one closer to Arlington so that Henry and Marsha could visit their aunt more frequently. He also arranged the move, which the older woman now agreed to.

Marsha and Henry feel upset that they did not act more quickly. Henry tells me that he's repeatedly asked himself, *Would I have behaved any differently if this were my mother instead of my aunt?* He can't answer that question, but he doubts that he would have been able to take a leave of absence, even to care for his own mother. The couple finds solace, however, in knowing that they did not let their suspicions lie, and that there was someone to help out when help was needed. They feel (and events proved them right) that, although she lived at some distance from them, ultimately Aunt Mae was not alone.

A good way to begin a search for a geriatric care manager is to contact the National Association of Professional Geriatric Care Managers, an organization based in Tucson, Arizona, that began with 30 members in 1986 and has grown to more than 650 members nationwide, for names of members in the area where your parent lives. Elder-law attorneys, social workers at hospitals and senior centers, and counselors available through employee assistance programs can also make recommendations.

Once you make the contact, check the credentials of the case manager. Ask to see if he's licensed or certified. Ask how long he has been in private practice, whether he's available twenty-four hours a day, how he charges (by the hour or by the project), and whether there are any hidden costs (such as telephone and travel time). Request references. Check with the Better Business Bureau to learn whether complaints have been registered against the company. Finally, trust your instincts. Does the care manager's personality mesh with yours? Can you be open and honest with this person? The more comfortable you are with the professional you hire to stand in your stead, the better you'll feel about managing this admittedly difficult situation.

When You Are the Distant, Less-Involved Caregiver . . .

This chapter has focused on the long-distance caregiver who, in spite of geography, still struggles to be a major player in the care of a parent. There are others among the children of aging parents who live at a distance and are much less involved in parent care. Perhaps they rely on a sibling who is providing the major care, or on other relatives who live near the parent. There may be a history of discord between parent and child, or perhaps the parent's illness has led to some estrangement between brothers and sisters, leading the faraway caregiver to further distance himself from the goings-on. If you are that less-involved caregiver, and you're reading this book, chances are that you'd like to play a more active role. Consider the following:

There are many ways for a long-distance caregiver to be involved in a parent's care. For example: You can offer to take charge of financial matters, to do your parent's taxes if he or she is no longer able to manage the task.

If you want to reach people, services, or programs in your parent's community, you'll find it helpful to obtain a copy of the local phone directory, one containing a classified section. You can do *a lot* on the phone. Be prepared for a runaround, however. Keep careful records of the date and time a call is made, the name of the person with whom you speak, and the follow-up.

If your parent suffers from a specific disease or disability, you can do some research on the condition and pass the information along to the sibling who's more integrally involved in your parent's care.

You can join a support group, both to learn more about your parent's condition and to share your feelings with others who may be in the same boat.

Most important, you can make yourself available to your parent and to the primary caregiver. If a mother or father is able to travel, it's a good idea to have the parent come for a visit. Use the time to renew and reshape the relationship. Having a parent visit is also a way of providing the more involved caregiver with some much-needed time off. If the parent is unable to travel, then make the trip to the parent's home, for exactly the same reasons.

Long-distance caregivers who are not involved in regular parent care can still contribute financial support. They can still provide emotional support by calling and *listening* to the parent and by bolstering the efforts of the primary caregiver: brainstorming with her when that is wanted, offering advice when it is requested, expressing appreciation.

The question of how to participate in a parent's care when you live three hours or three thousand miles away has no simple or perfect solution. Fortunately, there are programs and people who can make the job somewhat easier for you, and ways in which you can become involved. "Distant" need not be defined as "detached." Long-distance caregivers, in particular, may need to give themselves credit for what they *are* able to accomplish rather than dwell on their failings and frustrations.

To review, then, those faced with the challenge of long-distance caregiving find the following helpful:

- placing calls to check up on the parent and reassure themselves;
- paying visits to the parent as frequently as circumstances permit;
- identifying a trusted observer who will check in with the frail elder;
- networking services and service providers within the parent's community;
- arranging for programs, like Meals on Wheels, to meet the older parent's nutritional requirements;
- taking advantage of family leave opportunities at work if and when necessary;
- utilizing the services of the local Office on Aging;
- signing on with a telephone assurance program;
- enrolling a parent in a friendly visitors program;
- employing a geriatric care manager or elder-law attorney to assess, and assist, in meeting a parent's needs;
- becoming knowledgeable about the parent's illness or disability;
- offering help with financial matters;
- joining a support group;
- serving as a source of support to the parent and to the primary caregiver.

Long-distance caregivers will also find it useful to get in touch with the Eldercare Locator, a nationwide service administered by the National Association of Area Agencies on Aging to help families find information about resources for older people in their community—services such as home-delivered meals, transportation, legal assistance, housing options, recreation and social activities, adult day care, senior center programs, home health services, elder abuse prevention, and nursing homes. The national toll-free number is (800) 677-1116. Have the following information ready when you call: the name and address of the older person (most important, the zip code to aid in identifying the nearest information and assistance sources) and a brief description of the problem or type of assistance you are seeking.

In addition, it is always useful to have the following information about your parents at hand: date of birth; social security number; Medicare or Medicaid number; health insurance information; lists of any medications they are taking; names, addresses, and telephone numbers of doctors, hospitals, and clinics involved in their medical care. As you will see in the next chapter, which deals with financial and legal matters, it is useful to have copies of a living will and power of attorney, as well.

CHAPTER 6

FOCUS ON FINANCES: REALITY AND EMOTION

⧽⧼

A recently aired television commercial sponsored by an insurance company features a family at dinner—husband, wife, two school-age sons. The wife appears troubled. The conversation goes something like this:

Wife: "My mother can't continue to live alone. We'll just have to add on a room and ask her to move in with us."

Husband (unable to meet his wife's eyes): "I don't see how we'll be able to manage that. There's the children's education to consider. And we need to set aside some money for our own retirement. We've been negligent about doing that. I'm sorry, but we just aren't able to afford it."

"Grandma can have my room," mutters the older son, looking down at his plate. "It's okay. . . ."

• • •

This fictional scene highlights a concern that is shared by many viewers, and it is this: when our parents grow old, will we become responsible for their welfare, and will we be up to the job?

Money is both a serious and an emotional issue. And so, for as long as possible, many of us—parents and children—walk around it, fearing to raise a subject that threatens to disturb the precarious equilibrium upon which so many family relationships rest.

"One of the most stressful issues in caregiving is *not knowing* what your parents' financial situation is," says Grace Weinstein, a financial consultant and author of *The Lifetime Book of Money Management*. "Older people often do not want to share information with their adult children, don't want to admit that they need help, or don't want to say how much money they have. They don't want to relinquish their independence and the privacy they have guarded for years. It can be very difficult for a caregiver to know what needs to be done if you don't know what the actual situation is."

When candor is missing, confusion often reigns.

"Every time I would ask my father if he needed money, he would tell me not to worry, that he was managing just fine," says a fifty-nine-year-old man who lives at a distance from his father, an eighty-seven-year-old widower. "That's how he'd put it: 'I'm managing.' He continued to send my children gifts (a ten-dollar bill on their birthdays), so I let myself feel reassured that there wasn't a problem.

"One evening, I received a phone call from someone who

lives downstairs from my father. When a neighbor of your elderly parent calls, you can rest assured that it's not to convey good news. And it wasn't. The neighbor told me that my dad's electricity had been turned off. I hoped that my father had just neglected to pay his bill. What I found out, however, was much more unsettling. Dad's social security payment covered his rent, with little left over. Doctors' bills and medication for a variety of ailments had been using up his small pension and were steadily eating into his meager savings. There was, in fact, no money to speak of. Dad simply had been too proud to tell me that, and I'd been too respectful of his privacy to press him on the money issue.

"I finally spoke to him frankly about how much money he had, about how much I could contribute, and about which government programs, like Medicaid, we could apply for. It's the kind of father-son talk that should have taken place years earlier. I also arranged with the telephone, gas, and electric companies to notify me if a payment was missed so that I could respond before essential services were cut off."

All too often, the time that children learn the truth about their parents' finances is when there is a crisis. "If you can," says Grace Weinstein, "speak to your parents while conversation is possible. You need to make sure they have a will. You also need to ask if they have a bank account or accounts, and where the accounts are located. [It's not at all unusual for caregivers to learn that their parents have several accounts, for example, some of which they opened years earlier to get a bonus toaster, radio, or other giveaway, and then left in place to gather interest.] Have they made out a durable power of attorney? Do they have a safe-deposit box, and if yes, where do they keep the key? Do they have a cemetery plot? Where do they keep the deed?"

As long as your parents are capable of making their own choices, they can and should handle their own business affairs. It is helpful for the children to know, however, where parents keep important financial documents like mortgage statements, insurance policies, wills, investment certificates, and real estate and car titles. "It's also helpful to get the name of their lawyer, accountant, insurance agent, banker, and financial planner, if they have one," says Weinstein.

Addressing the Elders' Fear of Poverty

Sometimes it's important to talk to a parent if only to reassure the elder that there *is* enough money to meet his or her needs. Many people, as they age, see money going out but very little coming in, and become extremely anxious about the state of their finances. Their uneasiness is expressed in a number of ways.

One caregiver reports, "My mother obsesses over the fact that she doesn't have enough money to live on, although that is not the case. She refuses invitations to have lunch out with friends because, she insists, she can't afford it. I tell her that she can have lunch at the Ritz if she feels like it, but it does no good. She has become a virtual recluse, which puts a great deal of pressure on me to come by frequently and take her out."

Says another caring daughter, "My mother became fixated on having cash. I wanted her to have money in her handbag so that she would feel secure, but I didn't want her to have too much money because she was no longer able to handle it. I also noticed that she'd developed a habit of hiding money away in her purse, in her shoe bag, in the hamper. So, whenever I would leave money with my mother, it would not be a twenty-dollar bill, but twenty one-dollar bills. The amount was less important than that she have a pile of money. And both my sister and I would reassure her, 'You have money in the bank.' We didn't go into details; it was neither helpful nor necessary. We reassured her at the level she could understand."

There was a time, not so very long ago, when my husband, Noel, would pick up his office phone to hear his mother's anxious voice. "How soon can you come by?" she would ask him, adding, "There are bills that have to be paid." No matter that he had dropped in on his mother on his way home from work only two days earlier and had attended to the few financial matters requiring attention. When the pressures of work compete with the pressures of parent care, as they do for many of us at one time or another, it is sometimes difficult to find the time to "stop by." If at all possible, however, a quick visit to reassure a concerned parent may be a far simpler way to deal with this anxiety than repeated verbal reassurances that just don't register.

My mother-in-law has been anxious, too, about the considerable amounts of money being spent for the services of the home care aides whose help has become essential to her welfare. Each week, when she had to make out a check for services rendered, Mom would find some fault with the service provider. This one was too intrusive; that one disrespectful. What she was really saying, as she dismissed one woman after another, was: they really aren't worth all that money. It was the money that bothered her the most. And the fear, one that is shared by many older people: *Will my money run out before my life does?*

Noel dealt with Mom's concerns by taking over the task of paying the aides, albeit the checks continue to be drawn on his mother's account. For some reason, it was helpful to Mom not to have to make out the check—which was a concrete reminder, each week, of the expense involved in meeting her needs. (Since then, my mother-in-law has become more frail, less feisty. Noel would welcome a call from her now, chastising him for his failure to come by and take care of the bills. In a sense, we now look back at that period as "the good old days" when my mother-in-law was capable of complaining.)

Money as Power

Financial anxiety is common among the old and ailing. In a sense, it's not so much the money they're concerned about but the state of being dependent. So much autonomy is lost as an individual finds himself increasingly having to turn to doctors, to children, and to assorted caregivers to manage various aspects of his life.

A parent whose health and independence are waning may see money as the last vestige of power and be reluctant to let go. Some use money to manipulate their adult children, fearing that when the money is gone these same children will no longer be so attentive. Children who allow themselves to be manipulated play right into the parents' game. And nobody benefits.

Phillip Sherman found that out the hard way. Phillip was the constant son, the one who went straight from school into his father's business: "Vacuum Cleaners—Sales and Service."

Phillip married, moved near his parents' home and, after his mother died, had his father over for dinner every Sunday. A younger brother, Barry, went to college, became a lighting engineer, and moved to Seattle.

"My father was never an easy man to work for," says Phillip, now fifty-nine, "and I often thought about leaving him, but I didn't. For one thing, he needed me. For another, I told myself (and my father constantly reminded me) that I was building equity in the business—ten, twenty, eventually thirty-five percent. As my family's needs grew greater and my children became ready for college, I would periodically ask my father (I still had to ask!) for a raise in salary or a greater share in the business. Pop would turn me down, while repeatedly assuring me that, eventually, the business would be mine. He said that to me when I cared for him through three serious illnesses—colon cancer, heart surgery, and a major stroke."

Phillip and his wife, Annie, would visit his father every day, at home or in the hospital. They'd buy him groceries, see that he ate and make sure that, in general, his needs were attended to. Still, the relationship between the two men worsened. From time to time, from the depths of his pain and suffering, the father would threaten his son with disinheritance, even as that same son would take him to the bathroom. Says Phillip, "Then I would get a phone call from my brother, Barry, asking why I was causing Pop such aggravation. Apparently our father had been in touch with the favored but absent son. 'Why can't you just humor the guy?' Barry would say. 'Why don't *you* come home and humor him?' I would answer, knowing full well that Barry would never do that."

Six months ago, the father died, leaving his entire share of the business—65 percent—to Barry, who has effectively become Phillip's boss and who is unwilling to set the will aside. The matter is now in the courts, and the brothers no longer speak to one another. Says Phillip, "How's that for a father's legacy to his children!" He adds, "My father always told me, 'My word is my bond.' I should not have taken his word. As a businessman, I should have handled matters in a businesslike fashion."

Unfortunately, it is all too common for there to be discord between brothers and sisters over a parent's estate or assets . . . often initiated by the very same siblings who stood on the sidelines for years, doing nothing. "This may be a traumatic experience, especially when your own brother or sister is the antagonist," says Carl Eisdorfer, a geriatric psychiatrist and gerontologist at the University of Miami. In their book *Seven Steps to Effective Parent Care,* Eisdorfer and his longtime collaborator, Donna Cohen, strongly recommend that siblings work at building collaborative partnerships with one another, if at all possible, when parent care is required. "Working cooperatively with your brothers and sisters can make parent care a lot easier," they write.

If such cooperation is not possible, however, says Dr. Eisdorfer, "it's important that the caregiver not let himself get set up in a guilt situation, where he impales himself on the economics of caregiving. Caregivers have got enough other problems without having to be self-sacrificial in that area. Then you've got to come up with the most draconian of solutions, which is to find a helpful attorney specializing in family law."

It's also useful for the child who is most involved in a parent's care to keep scrupulous records of all money spent, both to be clear about any reimbursements that are necessary and to be able to explain to the siblings, if ever there's a question, just where the money went.

When it comes to caregivers and money, we are dealing with two different groups of people. There are caregivers who must provide financial support, and then there are caregivers whose parents have money and who must help manage the money. *These are two very different situations, with different tensions.*

The Money Crunch

Only a small percentage of the elderly (less than 5 percent) are reported as full dependents by their children. It is not uncommon, however, for adult children to contribute to their parents' care in a variety of ways: helping with the rent; paying for homemaker services; buying groceries; and so on. Allen Levine, assistant director of social services at Cancer Care, notes, "Often, a child may have to take time off from work to take Mom for chemotherapy or radiation. That affects the caregiver financially."

If you don't have much money and you have to help your aging parent, caregiving is more difficult—especially when a parent suffers from a serious or chronic illness, and you're overwhelmed by the parent's condition, by the care that is required, and by its high cost. "I think about money all the time now," I am told by a daughter whose bedridden mother requires round-the-clock nursing care. "Everything my father left, every bit of what was once a comfortable estate, is being depleted by Mom's illness, and I just don't have the money to pay for doctors, nurses, rehabilitation therapists, medication. I keep thinking, *What will happen when the money runs out?* I find myself hoping for a miracle—either I win the lottery or my mother goes quickly.

"Isn't that awful?" she adds.

It's awfully honest, I think, for I hear echoes of this statement, although they're often muted, in talks with many other caregivers.

"The money keeps going out," I'm told by Laura Wolensky, an only child and long-distance caregiver who is also the major supporter of two frail elderly parents. Laura's father, Elliot, ninety-two, is confined to a wheelchair, the result of a combination of ailments that have slowly enfeebled his body and are now overtaking his mind. Her mother, Harriet, eighty-seven, has developed a slight heart arrhythmia, a chronic bladder infection, and memory loss. In the past eight years, Laura's mother has experienced several episodes in which she has passed out. It's a condition known as Falling Down Syndrome, Laura has been told.

"I would speak to my mother on the phone," says Laura, "and her voice would sound funny. Slightly disoriented. And I would ask her if everything was all right. She would say, 'I don't want to go to a hospital.' Then I'd call her physician and he would say, 'What do you want? She's old.' I can't tell you how many times this has been said to me. I find it very hurtful."

There is much pain, for both Laura and her parents, in the realization that, indeed, they *are* old, and that they are now forced to look to her, their child, for emotional and financial support. "My father was an accountant with the Internal Revenue Service," says Laura. "He never earned a lot of money, but he wasn't a very big spender, either. I was my parents' one extravagance. They gave me anything I needed—braces, piano lessons, a college education that made it possible for me to become a teacher. When I married and had children, my mother offered to take care of them so that I could return to work. This underscores why, to this day, I feel a financial obligation to my parents.

"Very simply, my mother and father have outlived their savings," she says. "Now my own children are grown and married, my husband has retired and would like us to travel, but I can't leave my job because I need a regular income in order to pay for my parents' care. It costs me twenty-five thousand dollars a year."

The money goes to pay for Carla, a neighbor of the older couple, who does the grocery shopping for them, fixes their meals, drives them to doctors' visits, and generally sees to their care. A second helper works the weekend shift. "Everything costs a lot," says Laura. "I'm really scared because I sense that my parents will soon require round-the-clock care, and I just don't know how I'm going to manage that. I think my mother and father should be on some sort of public assistance, possibly Medicaid, but because I'm up north and they live in Florida, I have not been able to arrange anything. I want to do what's best for them and what's best for me, and I don't know what that is."

Seven months pass before I speak to Laura again. She informs me that her parents now live in a nursing home in Florida. "The hardest thing was making the decision to move my parents to a nursing home," she says, "but once the decision was made, I began to do some investigating. I learned that the cost of nursing home care in Florida was about half what was being charged for comparable facilities in New York—three thousand dollars a month as compared to six thousand dollars a month *per patient*—so I focused my search in Florida.

"Many of the places I visited were filled. They didn't have room for one of my parents, let alone two, and I wanted a place that would make it possible for my mother and father to be roommates. I finally found a nursing home that would do that, and we moved my parents in."

Money from the sale of their apartment covered the first several months of her parents' care. In the meantime, the social services director of the home guided Laura in applying for Medicaid for her parents, which picked up the bill once their money ran out. "We should have done this years ago," says Laura, who is at long last able to make plans for her own retirement.

Help Is Available

Medicare, Medicaid, entitlements, insurance forms . . . as a caregiver to an ailing parent, you very likely will find that you and your parent face massive expenses. *You have to know what's available to cover them.* You also have to learn about an array of programs and policies that, at best, can be described as daunting. With the complexity of tax laws and the Medicare/Medicaid situation, you've got to have help. Elder care lawyers, geriatric care managers, hospital outpatient specialists, administrators of senior residences, and admissions directors at nursing homes—all of these professionals work with these issues every day and can guide you. Use their services. *Don't try to go it alone.*

An understanding of some of the available programs may also be useful.

Medicare is a federal health insurance program available to people aged sixty-five or over and to certain disabled people regardless of age. Medicare covers home care for a short term and only under certain restricted conditions (such as blood pressure monitoring and surgical dressing changes). Except in a few situations, Medicare does not pay for nursing home care, unless it is ordered by a doctor and is for a limited time (for rehabilitation following a stroke, for example).

Medigap is private supplemental insurance that covers the portion of medical bills not paid by Medicare. Some Medigap plans offer additional benefits. Many doctors will accept the Medicare assignment, making supplemental insurance unnecessary. Medigap plans tend to be costly and are strongly promoted to the elderly population. As a caregiver, you will want to make sure that your parent has only one Medigap policy. Depending on your parents' situation, you may find this insurance useful.

Medicaid covers the cost of medical care for financially needy patients. The laws governing qualification for Medicaid are federally mandated, but they give states leeway in setting their own standards. Medicaid bases eligibility on two criteria: income and assets. Faced with the staggering costs of managing a chronic or debilitating illness, middle-income people often "spend down" their money on medical expenses or transfer their assets in order to qualify for Medicaid.

Many elderly people, and those who care for them, are reluctant to apply for Medicaid, even when (as Laura came to understand) it makes sense to do so. After a lifetime of self-sufficiency, they feel humiliated to have to turn to the government for help. But such help is not only necessary, it can be a lifeline for many families that find themselves confronted by the complex demands of old age and illness, not the least of which is the cost.

Caregiver Richard Lauffer credits his mother's physician, who heads a geriatric clinic at a major medical center, with setting him on the right path. Says Lauffer, "One of the first things the doctor said, after he told me that my mom had Alzheimer's disease, was, 'I recommend that every one of my patients get on Medicaid, no matter what the assets and financial situation, because the costs of this illness will eventually drain any assets you have.'

"Getting my mother on Medicaid was tough," says the caregiver, "but *keeping* her on Medicaid has been even tougher. There's so much bureaucracy and so many snafus. Granted that Medicaid workers are probably overworked, but the problems involved in dealing with the system can drive a reasonable person crazy. If anything goes wrong, if you fail to file a paper on time or to fill it out exactly as required, your parent loses her eligibility.

"For example," he continues, "we received a form on July twenty-third that stated it had to be filled out and returned by July twenty-third if my mother was to retain her eligibility. I responded at once, but it took a week for the letter to reach the appropriate office. The result: my mother was dropped from the program, and I had to battle to have her reinstated. So here's what I've learned: Don't send things through the mail. When you get an official paper, *fax* the response. Try to reach your caseworker and tell her to expect the fax. You may have trouble locating your caseworker. They're more often in the field than in the office, but call, leave messages, and fax."

When There's Money to Be Managed . . .

Obviously, older people who are financially secure, and their children, are spared the kind of tension that comes with worrying about how to pay for home care attendants, nurses, geriatric care managers, and a senior residence. The financial issues that engage caregivers in cases where there's sufficient money, perhaps even a good deal of money, are differently challenging, and are often frustrating in their own way. You have to know when to involve yourself in your parent's affairs.

Caregiver Marjorie Cooper tells her story. "My mother, in her early sixties when my father died, was left with lots of money, which was divided among many different investments. For the next fifteen years, she lived well and independently, becoming involved in charitable causes, traveling to Europe, spending time with my family or my sister's family, and generally enjoying life.

"Ten years ago, Mother was found to have a huge tumor in her uterus, which was successfully removed. Soon after, I began to notice signs that she was becoming forgetful. I mentioned it to her doctor, who said it was nothing to worry about. So I filed it away in my mind where, in time, it was joined by a growing list of strange behaviors that I noted but didn't really want to acknowledge until, one day, there was an incident that forced me to sit up and take notice.

"I was at work when I received a phone call from a stockbroker who is also a friend of the family. He said, 'Marjorie, get yourself up here. Your mom was just in my office with a five-thousand-dollar negotiable security.' She had removed it from her safe-deposit box and walked several blocks to the stockbroker's office to ask him what to do with it. Thank God she had gone to somebody we knew. He walked Mother back to the bank, helped her redeposit the security, and took her home. Then he phoned me to say, 'Get up here and empty the safe-deposit box.' So I got on a train that same afternoon. That's when I began to look after my mother's affairs.

"Mother didn't really have a handle on what she had. We had a lawyer come to her apartment while she was still able, and we changed her will (not its intent, but making it contemporary, with money going into trusts as appropriate). But the important thing at that time was that he told me about both the durable power of attorney and the durable power of attorney for health care [explained later in this chapter], and that was very helpful.

"My sister Bernice lives across the country, and I live two and a half hours away from Mother's home. In addition, we both have busy careers. Neither of us had the time or knowledge to oversee our mother's affairs. Through Mother's bank, we arranged for automatic payment of as many recurring bills as possible: rent, gas, electric, telephone. We then hired a financial manager, and met with him. We laid out our goals. We needed a certain amount of money to meet Mother's expenses, which now included paying a private agency for the services of a home-care attendant. We also needed the money to grow because we weren't sure of what Mother's future needs would be. We needed to amalgamate and simplify. The financial manager arranged to have everything put into a cash management account—you can write checks on it. His fee for managing my mother's account was one and a half percent of the total value of the portfolio. If he can increase the value of the portfolio, he gets more money.

"The point is," says Marjorie, "if you do have resources, you do need professional help. It's part of taking care of the person. You may not be qualified to be the investment banker, lawyer, or accountant for a parent, just as you can't be the doctor, dentist, or social worker. Caregiving is emotional, practical, and also financial. Doing the right thing for your parent, *and doing right for yourself,* involves getting the right kind of help on all fronts. Further, it cuts down on the possibility of friction between siblings, the likelihood that one will question the financial decisions made by the other. For me, that's reason enough to turn to a professional."

Caregivers who are called upon to assist parents in handling their financial affairs will find it useful to know about the following options.

If the parents' affairs are simple, a joint checking account may be the least complicated way to make it possible for a son or daughter to pay bills for parents when such intervention is required.

The *durable power of attorney,* which Marjorie found so helpful, is a legal document that allows a parent to delegate financial responsibilities to an adult child or other designated individual in advance so that, if the parent becomes mentally or physically disabled, guardianship won't be necessary. (Guardianship involves a legal proceeding whereby one person is designated the guardian of another and is given the authority to act in the other person's interest.)

The durable power of attorney gives the adult child—or other trusted agent—authority to withdraw funds from a parent's bank account, transfer stocks, and buy and sell property—in short, to manage a parent's financial affairs when the parent is no longer able or capable of conducting business as usual. This is especially important when there are medical bills, nursing home costs, and other extraordinary expenses to be paid.

A *durable power of attorney for health care,* also known as a health-care proxy, names a specific person to make health-care decisions if the adult patient is no longer able to do so. (A *living will* contains the adult's instructions about how the person wishes to be treated medically when no longer able to make his or her own decisions: whether the person wishes to be on a life-support system, to be resuscitated, and so on.)

"Durable" is the key word when power is delegated; otherwise, the power of attorney may be nullified if a parent becomes incapacitated.

"Copies of the durable power of attorney should be sent to banks, financial managers, anyone handling your parent's accounts," suggests Marjorie Cooper. "We learned that some banks and brokerage firms will not accept a general form, insisting on one of their own. They should be asked to respond *in writing* that the document has been received and accepted."

Another caregiver cautions, "Get many copies of the durable power of attorney, signed and notarized, because some institutions will want to keep the original." She speaks from experience. "I almost had to relinquish my only copy when I sold my folks' house for them," she says. "I then went up to the nursing home and got my father to sign another one, with a notary in attendance. My father's signature was sprawled all over the page. I think that's the last time he was able to sign his name to anything."

The importance of making timely arrangements is something that was brought home to our own family. My mother-in-law had reached a point at which it became important for her children, Joan and Noel, to manage her affairs for her. Brother and sister were in agreement on this, and they arranged to have a lawyer meet with them in their mother's apartment to explain to their mother what the document was and why it was needed. My mother-in-law listened respectfully, nodding in agreement, as the lawyer set forth the situation.

Toward the end of her presentation, the lawyer asked, "Do you understand the need for this document?"

"Yes, I do," said my mother-in-law clearly.

"And do you know the two people who will be empowered to make decisions for you should you be unable to do so?"

"Yes, of course," said my mother-in-law. "They are my son and my daughter."

"And will you now sign this document?" asked the lawyer, handing Mom a pen.

"I think not," said my mother-in-law distinctly, and stuck to her guns.

On another day, at another time, she did go along with the arrangement, a necessary one, but I will not forget the

look of exasperation on my husband's face when he returned home from that aborted effort. Obtaining the right papers *before* they were necessary could have avoided the
tension that he and his sister experienced at that time.

If your parent is reluctant to sign a durable power of attorney, you may want to suggest a *"springing" durable power
of attorney,* which becomes effective only if a parent is found
incapable of handling his or her own affairs. A court may
have to decide the parent's status, however, complicating the
issues for the caregiver at a time of crisis.

Living trusts, guardianships, conservatorships, and other
ways of managing money are best discussed by parent and
caregiver with a responsible professional.

Many advocacy groups and health-care organizations offer free clinics on financial and legal planning. Caregivers do
well to make time in their schedules to attend one of these
programs. As an informed caregiver, you will be better able
to advise your parents about any programs that might help
them and, in so doing, help yourself in the process.

In summary, then, the following actions can help caregivers
in dealing with the delicate issue of involvement in a parents' financial affairs, when and if such an interest is appropriate:

- knowing the parents' financial situation;
- taking over bill paying for an anxious parent;
- arranging with utilities for third-party notification of
  late payments;

- establishing a method for payment of as many recurring bills as possible;
- seeking professional advice about programs and policies that help the elderly meet their obligations;
- employing the services of a money manager;
- arranging for parents to qualify for Medicaid assistance, if appropriate;
- obtaining a durable power of attorney, and making sure to have many copies of the document;
- *planning ahead.*

Helping a parent deal with the costs of care imposed by illness and infirmity is a demanding task for many caregivers. And an emotional one, as well. This is, after all, the person who doled out your allowance, who surprised you with a bicycle on your birthday, and perhaps bought you your first car. Now you may find yourself confronting a reversal of responsibilities, and it is at best uncomfortable. The following chapter addresses this shifting of roles and its impact on the caregiver.

CHAPTER 7

MAKING DECISIONS FOR YOUR PARENTS

My sister, brother, and I are concerned. Mom should not be living on her own anymore, we think. Yet we are having trouble implementing any other arrangement because, whenever we raise the issue, our mother insists that she wants to remain in her own place, surrounded by her own things. She keeps repeating, "I have everything here." She then itemizes her assets.

"I have the center," she says, referring to a nearby senior center, once a mainstay of her social life, which she now seldom attends. "I have convenient shopping nearby"—also true, except that she often mislays her grocery list and returns home to find the refrigerator empty of the staples of her diet: orange juice, milk, and English muffins. Then she forgets to go back to the store. "I have my friends," she says. More than a year has elapsed since the last time a neighbor knocked on Mom's door.

Up to the present time, we have gone along with Mom's position, however uneasily, because we are loath to challenge our mother's waning self-esteem, her right to make decisions about the way she lives her life. But when do we conclude that we can no longer accede to Mom's wish to live independently? Do we have to wait for a disaster to happen before we go ahead and make this decision for her?

Complex and often subtle changes take place in relationships between parent and child as both grow older, including (in many cases) a shift in power from the parent to the child. Where for years the parent had been responsible for, and supportive of, the child, it is now the grown son or daughter who is called upon to become increasingly supportive of, and sometimes responsible for, the welfare of the aging parent.

The turnaround is made achingly clear in *Patrimony*, Philip Roth's poignant evocation of the last years of his father's life. The son writes:

> I then spoke four words to [my father], four words that I'd never uttered to him before in my life. "Do as I say," I told him. "Put on a sweater and your walking shoes."
>
> And they worked, those four words. I am fifty-five, he is almost eighty-seven, and the year is 1988. "Do as I say," I tell him—and he does it. The end of one era, the dawn of another.

Sons and daughters, we find ourselves shifting from *ask* to *order*, from *please* to *do it* in conversations with our frail elderly parents. We cajole, we confer, we direct, acting competent and confident, and wondering all the while if we're making the right decisions, doing the right thing. It is common to hear people speak of this transition as "parenting one's parent," but the concept is flawed. No matter how frail, how dependent our parents may be, they do not become our children. That's not a possibility.

Nor is it the adult child's role to make decisions for an aged parent but rather, insofar as it is possible and reasonable, to make decisions *with* a parent. We sometimes forget that, neglect to ask, are impatient to wait for an answer delivered with halting speech.

"The distinction is very important," says Amy Horowitz, director of the Lighthouse Research Institute. "It's not as if the parent is a new person who has entered your life [and whom you *can* direct]. This is someone with whom you have shared a lifelong relationship. . . . And that history cannot be ignored."

When the caregiving child assumes responsibility for managing aspects of a parent's life, says Horowitz, "it's not role reversal; it's a matter, for the child, of achieving filial maturity, which involves the acceptance of being dependable, and of being able to be depended on by your parent." In other words, it is an evolution, not a revolution, in the parent/child relationship.

A caregiving daughter has been busy from morn till dusk escorting her elderly mother on assorted errands: to see the doctor; have prescriptions filled; eat lunch; buy sturdy shoes; visit with an aunt who is ailing. When the daughter reenters her own home later that evening, she's greeted by her husband, who asks how she has spent the day. She answers, "I've been childing," by which she means that she was engaged in the kinds of things that an adult child is sometimes called upon to do with and for a parent.

Hearing the story, I am taken with the word. *Childing* is an appropriate description of what most adult caregivers do for their parents, it seems to me. *Parenting* is not. Childing may, but doesn't have to, include a challenging aspect of caregiving: the need for the grown son or daughter to be involved in making critical decisions that have an impact on the lives of their parents. Philip Roth aptly captured the feeling: it is an awesome alteration in a lifelong relationship.

Once engaged in decision making, adult children often face a dilemma between autonomy and paternalism: respecting a parent's right to remain independent versus knowing when and how to help. My friend Paula is just beginning to grapple with this problem. Paula is in her early forties; her parents are in their seventies. Paula tells me that she's concerned because her mom has been experiencing periods of forgetfulness lately, and the daughter fears that this may be a symptom of a more serious problem.

"I want to make an appointment for my mom to see a neurologist," Paula says, "but I don't know how to tell my mother that I've noticed her doing some irrational things. How do I explain to this proud woman what I think needs to be done?"

The quandary in which Paula now finds herself will ring true, with variations, for many children whose parents have begun to lose their powers. The children think:

- *This is Daddy, the man I've always looked up to. How do I step in now and tell him how to run his life?*
- *How do I look at my mother and tell her that she's lethal, that she ought not to be driving?*
- *How do I tell my dad, an accountant, that he should no longer be seeing clients because he makes so many mistakes?*
- *How do I suggest to my parents that they ought to be investigating retirement communities?*
- *How do I do that when my parents tell me they are fine?*

The inability to resolve these problems can leave the children feeling frustrated . . . helpless . . . guilt-ridden . . . responsible. We fear that if we don't step in quickly and decisively, the house of cards that protects our aging parents will come tumbling down. Says geriatric care manager Nick Newcombe, "Caregivers have to learn that you cannot solve every problem for a parent. You do the best you can, which includes taking some risks. The house of cards is often sturdier than you think. And if it does collapse, that's when you call 911 and get the help you need."

Taking a Reality Check

It is often hard for a son or daughter to make the assessment of when it is time to step in. You may be too close to the situation . . . or you may live too far away. When in doubt, it is helpful to turn to neighbors and friends, people who see your parent frequently, to find out if their observations corroborate your judgment. It can also be useful to seek a professional assessment, especially when you're faced with the need to intervene in such critical issues as management of a parent's financial affairs, health matters, and residential arrangements.

The need for intervention is but one factor to be considered. The second factor has to do with the recipient's accepting a child's involvement. Newcombe explains, "There are parents who make the transfer of responsibility easier for us. They do not fight our efforts. It's clear that they're relieved to be taken care of. The independent parent—the one who has been easier to deal with all along—often becomes more difficult when help is needed."

Some adult children find it easy to go ahead and make the decisions.

Most of us do not.

The Driving Dilemma

Driving is one of the first issues about which children become greatly concerned, because it is an area that can entail great risk. It is also one of the hardest activities for older people to give up because it involves their independence and their ability to get around. Driving tends to be one of the most important symbolic issues in terms of reworking the relationship between parent and child.

Knowing this, adult children are often reluctant to even raise the issue with their parents, although they worry about it a great deal—worry about the safety of their parents and about potential victims of any car accidents the parents might cause. You may recall Georgina Frost Adams (see chapter 4), who saw her fear become reality when her father wrecked his car, injured two people, and almost killed himself. Yet she still found it difficult to raise the issue and, even after she did, she could not get her willful father to give up driving a car.

Vivian Greenberg, an author and clinical social worker who specializes in the relationship problems of older adults and their families, suggests a way for children to address this issue with their parents. "Don't accuse them," she says. "Don't say, 'Dad, you're a dangerous driver.' Use 'I' messages instead: 'I really worry about your safety when you're driving now, Dad. You've had a few minor accidents and I'm afraid you might hurt someone or get hurt yourself.' "

There is no guarantee that such efforts will work, as Georgina Frost Adams learned when her father thanked her most kindly for her interest and then went out and bought a new car. If you find yourself meeting resistance from a parent, your only recourse may be to wait a while . . . and try again. Or you can call in replacements.

"Sometimes a parent will take advice better from a grandchild than from a child," says Judith Brickman, a coordinator with the Alzheimer's and Long Term Care Resource Center of the New York City Department for the Aging. "There's no generational conflict there. In other words, the older person thinks: If my granddaughter tells me that I ought to stop driving, it's because she loves me, she's concerned about me. If my daughter tells me the same thing, she wants to boss me around and doesn't want me to make my own decisions."

When there is clear and imminent danger, however, the caregiver has no choice but to act. A decision must be made and enforced with little delay and, often, with a great deal of pain for everyone involved.

"Getting my parents to give up their car was the most devastating thing I had to do," says a caring daughter. "My father had not sat behind a wheel for years. My mom was the one who used to drive the two of them shopping, to the social hall of their retirement complex, to church. Then Mom became too ill to be trusted with a car, her doctor said she should no longer be driving, and so I laid down the law. 'You have got to sell the car,' I told my parents in a tone that brooked no disagreement. It was a tone I'd been taught from childhood that I was never to use with my parents, who themselves had never imposed a similarly dictatorial edict on me. We went together and sold the car. It was the right decision, and yet I continue to feel so awful about it."

Financial Takeover

Finances are the second major area of conflict between parents and children, an area in which the risks are different than with driving but can also be great (see chapter 6). Ken Stevenson, a caring son and only child, still anguishes over his decision, reached with difficulty, to take over the payment of his mother's bills.

"Managing her finances has long been a source of pride for my mother," says the forty-nine-year-old, who shared his mother's pleasure in her competence. "My father was the kind of man who comes to mind when you hear the phrase 'head of the house.' He was a strong man who took care of everything. After he died, almost twenty years ago, Mother was very proud that she was able to manage her own affairs. The symbol of that achievement was balancing her checkbook.

"During a visit to my mother last year, I looked at her two checkbooks and saw that they were a complete mess. One was more than a thousand dollars off. She had paid Con Edison twice in one month, and neglected to pay her insurance premium. When I asked what had happened, she didn't have any explanation. She seemed addled and defensive. At that point, I felt I had to say, 'I'm going to take over your checkbook.' My mother really didn't want that to happen. She has called me three or four times since then, saying, 'You should send me my checkbook because I don't have any checks to write.' I explain our new system to her: she sends me her bills, and I pay them.

"I do worry that, by taking my mother's checkbook, I have removed from her a powerful symbol of independence and self-esteem," Ken admits, "but I don't see an alternative. It's a three-hour drive, one way, for me to visit my mother. If she and I lived near one another, if I didn't feel competing pressure to spend time with my wife and children, and if my work didn't require me to be out of town so often, I would never have taken her checkbook. I would have managed to visit each week or ten days, written out the checks, and had her sign them. I could have made it work in a way that allowed her to still feel in charge. But the reality is that she doesn't live nearby, and I'm not prepared to rearrange my life in order to see her once a week. I've made the choice."

Ken speaks as if there was only one choice, a difficult one that is causing him to feel a good deal of remorse about the decision he made for his parent. In fact, there are several alternatives that this caregiver might well have explored, among them hiring an accountant or a geriatric care professional (granted, at a cost) who would come by on a regular basis to oversee the payment of his mother's bills. The help of a neighbor or long-term friend might also have been enlisted.

Armed with these options, the son could have sat down with his mother, shared his concern about the management of her finances, and asked her how *she* might wish to handle the matter: by hiring a professional who would go over her bills with her and make the appropriate payments or by delegating responsibility to her son. He could point out the benefits and drawbacks of each plan. By involving his mother in the decision making, Ken might well have been spared the guilt he now feels. He might even have felt some satisfaction in enabling his mother to retain the pride of self-direction.

When the Problem is Depression

Loss of self-esteem, loss of health, loss of mobility, loss of employment, loss of status, loss of loved ones—the list of losses experienced by many older adults is sometimes lengthy and often overwhelming. It is not surprising, therefore, to learn that depression is a common problem among the frail elderly. A serious problem. The highest rate of suicide in America is among older men in their eighties, mostly widowers. Major depressions are not just mood changes; they are truly incapacitating.

What *is* surprising is how often the problem is ignored (*She's not sick; she's just depressed*) or misdiagnosed (as cardiovascular illness or dementia). Children who are concerned that a parent may be depressed should be alert to the following symptoms:

- feelings of sadness or irritability;
- decreased interest in activities;
- trouble in getting to sleep, or oversleeping;
- noticeable change in eating habits, such as loss of appetite or overeating;
- persistent fatigue or lethargy;
- low self-esteem or guilt;
- decreased concentration, or indecisiveness;
- clinging behavior;
- talk of suicide, thinking that life isn't worth living.

Many people become sad or irritable, lonely or lethargic, from time to time. That's normal. If you observe several of these symptoms in your parent, however, and if they persist for two weeks or longer, some action is warranted. This is the time when you must step in and make some decisions for your parent, if necessary, for both your sakes.

Matty Arnold, a caring daughter, is becoming a victim of her mother's illness. She is edgy and distraught as she speaks about the turmoil in her own life, brought about by changes in her mother's behavior. "My father died a year and a half ago," she says, "and that's where this story begins."

Before Matty's father died, her parents were an active, vital couple, enjoying their well-earned retirement. Matty's father had worked as a truck driver, a job that took him away from the family for long periods of time. "When my sister and I were growing up," Matty recalls, "our mother worked four hours a day as a teller in a local bank, kept house, cooked, cared for the kids, was active in volunteer activities, played mah-jongg. She *functioned.* She was the role model for my sister and me. In the last year and a half, she has withdrawn from people, refuses to get out of bed, and seems to have given up all will to live. It really hurts to see that."

Before her father died, Matty would speak to her mother daily, and would see her once a week. Now the mother phones the daughter, an accountant, at work several times a day. "This past Friday is typical," says Matty. "I'm at work when the phone rings. It's my mother, of course. She says, 'I'm calling to say good-bye. I can't get out of bed. I want to die.' Now how am I supposed to react to a call like that?"

Matty has already done more than most, has taken her mother to a doctor to make sure that there is nothing physically wrong with the seventy-eight-year-old woman, and has then accompanied her mother to see a psychiatrist. "He asked my mother how she was and she said, 'I'm fine.' She's fine for everyone but my sister and me! I'm at a point where I don't know where I am anymore. The issue for my mother is to get out of bed every day and find someone to talk with. The frustration is that the doctor says she's fine. I'm at my wits' end. I just want my mother to be happy, and I don't understand why she's not."

Matty would do well to trust her intuitive feelings that her mother is *not* fine, and to seek another doctor in order to ensure that her mother gets the proper diagnosis and treatment. It's a task that is easier said than done; the supply of geriatric specialists is far less than the demand for doctors who are trained to diagnose and treat the needs of the elderly. It's a serious situation on many counts, but especially where depression is concerned, for the illness is not just an expected part of old age. Depression is serious and, in most cases, it is treatable.

Such antidepressant drugs as Prozac, Zoloft, or Paxil have proven very effective in treating the symptoms of depression, with far fewer deleterious side effects than were caused by older drugs. Nonetheless, a good deal of trial and error remains necessary. Says a caregiver whose parent is being medicated for depression, "You worry. Does the medicine have to be changed? The dosage adjusted?"

There are times when support groups take on the appearance of a pharmacologists' convention as adult sons and daughters speak with astonishing familiarity about this or that medication, its benefits and side effects. Because each of the drugs has advantages and drawbacks, it is helpful for caregivers to discuss them and compare notes, then raise questions with the parent's doctor. Psychological intervention is another useful tool in helping parents, like Matty's mother, deal with their grieving.

Interceding When a Parent Has a Serious Illness

Questions of candor and autonomy take on great urgency, as well, when a parent becomes ill with a debilitating or life-threatening illness. Doctors have been known to be paternalistic when it comes to older people, sharing information with the children that properly belongs to the parent, and leaving sons and daughters to wrestle with the decision: should the parent be told?

I have been there. With my siblings and mother, I have held corridor consultations with doctors outside the hospital room where my father lay dying of cancer of the bladder while we, his family, struggled to resolve the question, *What do we say to Pop?* We did not use the word *cancer.* We did not speak about the preciously short time left for my father to be in our midst. Instead, we decided to pretend to him that the operation had gone well, and that recovery was the task at hand.

With smiles on our tear-stained faces, we reentered his room and began the game of Hide the Truth, a game in which he, too, was a player. For my father was a very smart man, and we are convinced that, like us, he knew the reality of his situation. Like us, he kept quiet in order to spare his loved ones from facing the terrible truth. Like us, he was kept from reaching out, was denied an opportunity to say what was important to the people he loved.

As a result of this experience, I vowed that I would never again decide for my parent what she had a right to know about her own self, her own condition. And so, when my mother was discovered to have cancer, that information was shared with her, as was our family's joy at her recovery. Now that she has "memory problems," we talk about that, too. She tells me that she is frightened by her failing memory, and asks if the doctors can do something about it. Yes, I agree, it must be a terrible feeling. I tell her (gently, clearly) that there is as yet no cure for her illness, but that her children will help her and, as a family, we will try to deal with it as best we can. And we do.

Further, "the adult child must realize that the parent has a right to know about his condition and to make the decisions—for example, for or against a given treatment," says social worker Allen Levine of Cancer Care. "Some of the chemotherapies have serious side effects. Sometimes a child wants to go with the most aggressive treatment, and the parent says, 'Enough's enough.'"

Caregiver Sandra King ran into the opposite situation. Her father, a man in his late seventies, suffered from "sundowning," a kind of dementia in which he would become extremely agitated and irritated as the day's light faded. When the father was hospitalized, lights were kept on day and night in his room.

"There was no love lost between me and my father," says Sandra, "but I did take care of him during his illness and I thought I was very clear about his wishes, which went beyond 'do not resuscitate' to 'do nothing extraordinary.' Yet when I was asked by the doctors, 'What do you want us to do in terms of your father's care?' I was floored. I found that I couldn't make a decision for him. I just couldn't take that responsibility. So one bright and sunny morning, I spoke to my father, spelling out the options. I asked him, 'Dad, what do *you* want?'

"'Tell them to do everything possible for me,' he answered. I was shocked. But there it was, what *he* wanted. I told the doctors to do everything possible for him and they did, right up to his very last minutes on this earth. *The weight was off my shoulders.* The decision was his. And I have felt fine about it ever since."

In short, when decision making is called for, the adult child can find strength in:

- respecting the parent's autonomy;
- sharing decision making with the parent;
- being a dependable caregiver;
- accepting the necessity of risk taking;
- using "I" messages when talking with a parent;
- finding others to corroborate your judgment;
- involving grown grandchildren as intermediaries;
- enlisting professional help when appropriate;

- locating a knowledgeable doctor;
- being candid;
- stepping in when there's clear and imminent danger.

The need for the adult child to step in for a parent whose gait has become unsteady is a source of caregiver stress. The loss of a powerful parent is difficult to accept. This emotional aspect of caregiving is addressed in the chapter that follows.

CHAPTER 8

LOSS AND MOURNING

My mother has been sifting through the memorabilia of a life well lived, including letters from family and friends long gone; certificates of appreciation for her volunteer work on behalf of numerous charitable organizations; awards presented in recognition of her tireless efforts to raise funds in support of the State of Israel. On one of my visits to her, I find papers and plaques strewn across the dining-room table. I begin to gather them together, to make order out of chaos, when Mom stops me. "Look," she says, shaking her head from side to side. "It's hard to believe . . . I used to be somebody."

"You certainly were," I answer.

Then there is silence as each of us looks back.

I can only guess what goes on in my mother's mind, but I am able to share with you the images that go tumbling, one over the other, in mine.

CARING FOR YOURSELF WHILE CARING FOR YOUR AGING PARENTS

162

I see a woman who rose early each morning to prepare
breakfast for three children, sent them off to school, and
then boarded a bus that would take her to work. While my
father held down a salaried job, my mother managed our
family's hope for the future—"the store," a narrow retail shop
offering a wide variety of low-cost merchandise: handbags,
hosiery, costume jewelry, and luggage, the latter stacked on
shelves closest to the ceiling and accessible only by steplad-
der. Mom lived in the hope that no prospective customer
would come in and ask to look at a suitcase until after six in
the evening, when my father would arrive to relieve her.

At some point, my father left his job and my parents
worked in the store together, Monday through Saturday,
Mom still leaving at six and Pop staying on till nine o'clock,
at which time he would set the burglar alarm and draw the
iron gate across the storefront, marking the end of another
business day. On Sundays, my parents always held an open
house where, each week, family and friends would congregate to talk politics, play pinochle, and eat the broiled fish,
boiled chicken, and raisin-noodle pudding that were main-
stays of my mother's menus. If Mom wasn't a great cook, she
was at least consistent.

Mom was in her late fifties when my father died. I was
expecting my second child. My mother was not a hands-on
grandmother, and I was not the most dutiful of daughters.
We were occupied, I with my family and work, Mom with
her friends and volunteer activities. Life was full for us both.

Etched in my memory, however, is a phone call that I
made to Mom during this time. "I just called to tell you that I
love you," I remember telling my startled mother.

"Why all of a sudden?" Mom asked, laughing in surprise
and, I sensed, some embarrassment.

"Well, I was out with a group of friends last evening," I explained, "and all of the women complained about their mothers, who they said were constantly calling them to task for not phoning or visiting as often as the mothers would like. My friends feel pressured by their mothers' unending demands on their time. I love you because you have never made me feel guilty for not calling or visiting."

"That's because I understand," said my mother. "Of course I'm lonely sometimes and would like to see you more often. But just as I had my busy time in life, I know that this is your busy time. You have your husband, your children, your work, your friends. Do what you have to do and don't feel guilty." And I didn't. Not then.

This is the same woman who now asks me, in every other phone call, "Please tell me. Is there something that I should be doing that I'm not doing? Because I want to do the right thing and I just don't remember what that is. Isn't that terrible," she adds.

My mother and I are both mourning the "somebody" that Mom used to be.

Another tale of loss and mourning . . . At a dinner party, I find myself seated next to Paul, a slim, attractive man in his late forties who, I quickly learn, is an international lawyer. I enjoy hearing about some of the issues Paul deals with and the places he has visited. I don't recall how the conversation takes a turn from professional to personal, but it does, and suddenly Paul is talking to me about his parents. His voice is low, as if sharing a confidence.

"I remember when I received the offer to join my law firm," Paul tells me. "Although it seemed to be a great opportunity, it meant that I would have to pick up and move to Washington, D.C., from a town where I knew everyone. I wasn't sure I wanted that. So I phoned my parents to talk the matter over with them. That is how it always was in our family. I never made major decisions without consulting my mother and father. After my father died, and even after I married, I continued to phone my mother for her opinion. Mother had always been a very vibrant, thoughtful person. I could bounce possibilities off her and she'd help me think matters through.

"Slowly, however, I began to notice changes in my mother's behavior that foretokened later changes in our relationship. I would find myself telling Mother about a problem I was facing and, instead of asking me how I felt about it or what my options were, questions that I would have expected from her, she'd say, 'Oh, I'm sure everything will be fine.' She would then turn the conversation to the subject of her health. Mother had health problems throughout her life, but she had always been strong in fighting them. In recent years, she's gone downhill and has become fairly obsessive about her health. There was a period when I was angry about that. Now I'm learning to accept it."

In fact, it's clear that Paul is still trying to come to grips with the reality of his mother's altered state.

"The change in my mother has been very much on my mind of late," he says, "because the situation at my firm is no longer as stable as I'd like it to be, and I've been wondering whether to make a move. Many's the time I find myself instinctively reaching for the phone, wanting to talk to my mother about this, but then I stop myself because I realize that Mother's no longer able to support me in this way. I have found myself of late feeling a mixture of love and irritation toward my mother. She's eighty-four now, losing her grip on reality, and I have to be there for her instead of the other way around.

"The fact is," says the troubled son, "I want the mother I always had."

The most common difficulty among adult children seems to be realizing and accepting the waning powers of the aging parent. Physical handicaps, sensory losses, or mental impairment of the parents all become losses to the adult child, as well.

Our grieving begins from the moment we recognize that something is wrong. We're distressed by the decline of our parents' physical powers. "It's very painful to watch my mother, who was a human dynamo, not be able to do the things she did," says a sixty-year-old daughter. In dealing with diseases that steal the mind of the parent who was our anchor, we lament the loss of support and companionship. "Loneliness is something I walk with every day; emptiness is a constant companion," says a daughter who has spent the last four years caring for a mother who is no longer capable of recalling her name.

As a parent begins the slow descent into illness and incapacity, the adult child begins the process of mourning. "You mourn all the stages of life with your parent," says Allen Levine of Cancer Care. "You mourn Mommy, Mom, Mother, the good and the bad, what you had from your parent and what you didn't have." You mourn a parent to cheer you on or see you attain your goals. You mourn the loss of a vital, able grandparent for your children.

The Long Good-Bye

Often people analogize caring for an aging parent to tending to the needs of their children: "Well, I raised four kids, so I guess I can take care of my dad."

It's not the same. Says a geriatric counselor, "Children grow up, get better, get bigger, get stronger, become more self-sufficient, and need you less. Plus, you have the satisfaction of seeing them grow. Sometimes, parents need help for a short time and they, too, get better. But parents suffering from chronic illness tend to grow worse and need you more. Further, you have the pain of witnessing their deterioration."

We mourn the deterioration. The long good-bye that accompanies chronic illness or incapacity is often more painful, more difficult for the adult child to manage, than the grief that follows the finality of a parent's death.

In an attempt to come to grips with my own feelings of loss and mourning, I have found myself turning to the classic writings of Elisabeth Kübler-Ross, whose work with the critically ill and their families compels us all to look at the process of dying in a much more open and honest fashion. Dr. Kübler-Ross likens the reaction of family members confronted with a chronic or terminal disease of a loved one to the stages of adjustment experienced by the patient.

At first, she explains, there is likely to be *denial* ("Not my parent; the diagnosis must be wrong"), which is often marked by visits to other doctors in search of a second and third opinion.

This stage is followed by *anger* that this should be happening to your parent ("It's too soon; it's not fair—my mother [or father] is such a good person; it's too awful") and, further, that this should be happening *to you.* ("I want the mother I always had.") Many family members project their rage onto doctors, nurses, therapists, and home attendants. Many lash out at siblings and spouses. Some take their anger out on themselves. When dealing with a parent who we feel is in the process of leaving us (emotionally or physically), adult children often find that there is more than enough anger to go around.

Next, our mourning enters the stage of *bargaining*, as we find ourselves moving toward an acceptance of the unacceptable. Little by little, we adjust to what shocks us, learn how to live with the present situation, how to accommodate ourselves to its demands, because that often seems preferable to what it presages: the dread of what's next to come and the fear that neither our parents nor ourselves may be up to its challenges.

"I used to be annoyed when my mother would say, in every conversation, 'How's the weather up north? It's beautiful here,'" says a worried daughter. "Now she no longer asks, and it makes me very sad. Mom's home-care aide thinks it's a plus that my mother stopped repeating herself, but I got used to the repetition, and I see my mother's silence as further withdrawal."

Another daughter, a supercaregiver, confesses, "The thing that bothers me is not so much losing the mother I had, but not liking the woman I see emerging. Growing up, I don't remember regarding my mother as demanding, but lately she has become increasingly self-absorbed: the self-centered, spoiled, youngest child in the family that she must have been once upon a time. Each of these personality revelations is a shock; then I get used to it . . . until the next shock."

Seeing her mother in this light, realizing that the older woman is likely to become only more difficult and more dependent with the passing days, this caregiver then enters a fourth stage: *depression.* Hope is gone; feelings of irritation are replaced by a great, pervasive sadness. In this stage, reaching out to others becomes critically important.

However difficult they have been, these stages move us toward an *acceptance* of the situation ("This is the way things are"), which ultimately permits us to grieve and to share our parent's grief at the unavoidable loss of self and, eventually, life. We have to give our parents permission to talk about their own fears and feelings of loss.

In the beginning, for example, when my mother would bemoan the loss of her faculties, I'd react by either changing the subject or denying the reality of what she was experiencing. She would mention the growing frustration of becoming hard of hearing and I'd chastise her for not wearing her hearing aid *instead of* commiserating with her about how it feels to find that she has to struggle to hear, and *then* suggesting to her that she might find a hearing aid helpful. When she complained about her failing memory, I'd bring up examples of things that she did remember to do, as if to prove her perceptions wrong (and perhaps assuage my own concern as well?). Now I listen. "I wish I could help you," I say.

"I know," says my mother.

Ways to Handle Our Mourning

In addition to acknowledging our grief and gaining an understanding of the different stages of mourning, we can take other, affirming actions. Instead of dwelling on loss, for example, it helps to focus on what the parent can still do, what he or she can still appreciate, and on what parent and child are still able to enjoy together. Building on strengths lessens the caregiver's frustrations.

Take the time to talk with your parent, adult to adult, to be real, authentic, empathic, and honest. Therapist Vivian Greenberg refers to this type of sharing as "finishing well." Often, she points out, the past is much more vivid to an aged parent than the events of yesterday. Take this time to ask your parent about the past, about her childhood, about how she felt as a young bride, as a young mother. When your parent is gone, there will be no one to hand this legacy to you and your children.

"It's important for the child to use this time to get the issues out," says caregiver Georgina Frost Adams. "When my mama died suddenly, a lot of stuff was left unsaid. I found myself grieving over the missed opportunities for communication. Since then, I have interviewed my daddy on audiotape. I did the same thing with my grandmother. I just talked about their life pretty chronologically. In my father's case, I rather think he enjoyed it; it kind of brought us closer together.

"Daddy and I have Sunday lunch together and we would sometimes sit outside and do the interview," the daughter says. "We talked a lot about Daddy's work, but it also helped to find out some stuff about myself: what I was like as a child, what our relationship was through his eyes. I never thought about it until this minute, but I think that was part of what I was working on—to feel a certain closeness and to reconstruct some of our relationship or to understand it in some way. At the end of his life, to sort of get a handle on that. Physically, we were sitting there close together, and the sun was shining, and there was a way to connect around some neutral issues and some very personal ones, and I think it has been very positive for both of us."

Join a support group. "The basic work of support groups is to deal with matters of grief and bereavement," says Rea Kahn, coordinator of support groups for the Alzheimer's Association. "When someone talks about Mother being incontinent, what's being talked about? You're talking about the fact that Mother's no longer a person who has the competence to go to the bathroom, and you mourn the loss of that function. So the theme is always separation, and grief, and bereavement, in my mind."

She offers as an example a support group that is mostly comprised of adult child caregivers who are at the early stages of the parent's illness. Says Kahn, "There's also a woman, Daphne, whose mother is in a nursing home. When Daphne talks about her feelings and experience, the other members of the group shiver because they're not there yet. I asked them, 'Has anyone wondered why Daphne is in this group?' Several people answered that they had. Daphne is like a spearhead for them. She's dealing with both physical and emotional separation, whereas they're mostly dealing with the emotional aspect. *So the theme is separation.* Everyone's on a different space along that continuum, but they're all dealing with separation from the person who was. The support group helps them to grieve that loss." (See chapter 2 for additional information on support groups.)

Seek counseling. Talking about feelings with a competent counselor (social worker, psychologist, psychiatrist, or member of the clergy) can be very useful in helping caregivers work through the grieving process and reach some kind of peace.

For long-distance caregiver Wilma Brody, seeing the right

professional at the right time turned out to be critical. Alzheimer's disease had been robbing Wilma's mother of her memory and ability to function as an independent woman. The change was particularly hard for Wilma, a highly successful businesswoman who had always viewed her mother as a role model, someone larger than life.

"As my mother began to slip further and further away from me," says Wilma, "I began to gain more and more weight, so much weight that I finally went to see a therapist about it. In the second session, the therapist had me go back into my childhood, where I saw my mother. For the first time, I understood that I had lost her. And I cried and cried. There *is* that moment when you must accept that the parent whom you knew is no longer there for you, even though she is still alive."

Wilma continues, "I will tell you that the cry with that therapist was the most pathetic thing that ever happened to me. I really mourned. And I was so surprised by it. I didn't realize how empty I'd been feeling—it was an emptiness that I had been trying to fill up with food. I mourned the loss of my powerful mother, and it was really helpful."

When adult children are no longer able to look at a parent as a pillar of strength, when parental needs have an impact on the parent's ability to nurture, these same children find that they must lament the loss. It helps if we then turn to others—spouse, in-laws, uncle, or aunt—for the love and support that sustains us through good times and bad.

Mourning is a painful and necessary process. Adult children can be helped to manage their grief, and not let it take over, by:

- acknowledging their feelings;
- appreciating the parent's abilities while regretting the decline in his or her strength and capabilities;
- using caregiving time to talk with a parent;
- sharing emotions with siblings and other family members who can provide comfort during the difficult times;
- joining a support group;
- seeking professional counseling.

In order to be able to cope with loss, caregivers need to have compassion for their parents and for themselves. Just how far the adult child is willing to go in meeting the day-to-day needs of an ailing parent is a matter for further consideration, one that is dealt with in the following chapter.

CHAPTER 9

KEEPING THE FOCUS CLEAR

By her own description, Beverly Williams is a family-centered person. "I grew up in a home where it was the norm for everyone to keep in touch," she says. "My mom used to talk to her parents and sisters every day; my father would check in with his parents just about as often. There was a constant back and forth of phone calls and visiting. So that is what I was used to and what I wanted for my own life."

Shortly after Beverly moved to Tempe, Arizona, with her husband and their two children, her parents bought a retirement home nearby, where they would enjoy the fall and winter, returning east to spend the spring and summer months with their two other grown children. Beverly's father suffered from Parkinson's disease, a progressively deteriorating neurological ailment, for sixteen years and found it easier to get around in a warmer climate.

"For much of that time, my mother was able to handle his care, so up until nine years ago my role as a caregiver wasn't very significant," says the forty-eight-year-old daughter. "Then Mom had a stroke, which severely affected her left side, and the family had to shift gears to care for both my father and mother. Dad was getting progressively worse, whereas Mom's illness presented new challenges that needed to be addressed.

"My mother, sister, brother, and I conferred (Dad had lost much of his ability to make decisions by then), and agreed that Mom would stay in the house in Tempe year-round. (Mom was so exhausted from the demands of caring for my father for all of those years that she finally accepted the fact that she now needed to concentrate on taking care of herself.) Dad would enter a nursing home in the area.

"That was a difficult transition. There was guilt. You look at a man whom you love dearly, someone who had been very successful in running his own business, and you have to make the decision to place him in a nursing home. Then you have to come to terms with the fact that this is the best you can do." As caregiving increasingly consumes her time and emotions, Beverly has managed to become adept at keeping the focus of her efforts clear.

"But life goes on," she says. "I would check in with my father at the nursing home daily. On Sundays, which came to be known as 'Parents' Day' around our house, I would arrange for him to be driven to our home, so he could join my mother, in-laws, and immediate family at dinner. Initially, I felt stressed about how this was going to work out. I understood that my kids did not always welcome the routine, that on certain Sundays they would have preferred for us to be alone as a family. Then I woke up one day and said, "Wait a minute. I absolutely adore my parents, and this is exactly what I want to do. And we will all just have to get along."

"I made it plain to my family that this was not an option, it was not a burden. I also made it clear that I needed and expected their cooperation, that either my kids or my husband would have to be around on Sunday afternoons to provide physical assistance with managing my father in his wheelchair. That required some coordination of schedules, and sometimes it was difficult because people wanted to go play tennis or basketball. However, I was not about to be tugged in both directions, with kids making demands on one side and parents pulling in another. What helped was that I was strong enough to declare that this was the way it was going to be for our family, and I did so in a way that brooked no dissension. Whether the conflict is between caregiver and spouse or caregiver and children, you have to set your priorities and make them clear. All in all, I feel that this has been good for my children and for us as a family."

Two years ago, Beverly's father died. Six weeks after, her mother suffered a second stroke, which mainly affected her ability to remember names and places. Beverly hired a woman to help her mother with such chores as cooking, cleaning, and grocery shopping. The daughter phones her mother each morning and evening and spends every Wednesday with her, when she pays the older woman's bills, accompanies her to doctors' visits, and does whatever else is necessary.

And, of course, there are those Sundays. "I'm sure that Mom would like me to come by more often," Beverly says, "because as our mothers age, everything becomes something that needs to be done immediately, but I've learned to accept that there are limits. I will always be there for my mother when she needs me, but I don't think I do either one of us a favor by being at her beck and call."

There's a fine line between dedication and martyrdom, between selflessness and self-preservation when it comes to caregiving, and Beverly seems to have found it. There is no question that at this time caring for a frail older parent is a priority in her life. But, the daughter is quick to add, "I have made *myself* a priority, too."

She explains, "There were times when I didn't do that, when I would find myself running over to see Mom almost every day and feeling guilty on the days when I stayed away. As a result, I was constantly feeling tired and stressed. I had no energy. The most important thing I have done for myself is to acknowledge the stress, and then work out a way to deal with it. One way I've done that is to set up some rules about what is important to me, like making time to exercise every morning. I belong to a 'walking group' that includes some wonderful women who are dealing with problems similar to mine. As we walk, we talk honestly with one another and help each other out. We also do a lot of laughing. That's been a tremendous salvation for me."

Examining Your Motives

Caring for an aging parent evokes a lot of feelings for adult children about what they are doing for that parent and why. Researchers Amy Horowitz and Lois W. Shindelman investigated the reasons that led families to provide care for their older relatives. Not surprisingly, affection (such as the love that Beverly feels for her mother) was among the reasons most frequently given by caregivers.

Reciprocity was another oft-cited response. (*My dad was always there for me. . . . Mom took care of my children so I could go to work. . . . My parents gave us the down payment on our house. . . .*) In such cases, the researchers note, the older parent enters the caregiving relationship with "credits" earned. Providing care when it is needed is a way for the adult child to give something back to a parent who has given so much.

Familial obligation is a third major motivator. Obligation need not be tied to affection. "Why do I continue to provide care to my mother?" asks a son in his early forties who has not enjoyed a mutually caring relationship with his mother, now suffering from dementia and other ailments. "*Dutiful* is really the term for it. Here is my mother, a person who is constantly belligerent and negative, and yet we are so involved in her care. My wife and I explain to our daughters, who are aged eight and five, that we take care of Grandma because she is ill and because this is what children should do for mommies and daddies when they need help. When parents have an illness, as difficult as it is, we have to try to make it better for them, we say. I think the term 'dutiful' is what you instill in yourself as much as you try to instill it in your children. So that's why I do it. That's why I give care."

Role modeling for one's own children is a fourth motive that is frequently mentioned. Other reasons include: to gain the parent's love; to make up for the past; to be one-up on your siblings; to gain respect from the community; and to inherit the parent's money. The motives for involvement may be as diverse as the care providers and their history with the older person.

When You Don't Get Along with Your Parent . . .

Researchers Horowitz and Shindelman found (and my own interviews have borne this out) that grown children and other relatives provide care regardless of whether they feel close to the care receiver. However, the more affection that exists between the caregiver and the person being cared for, the less negative are the feelings that accompany the provision of care. In other words, it is less stressful to provide care when you're doing it out of love than when obligation is the prime motivating factor and dislike the dominant emotion.

Caregiver Eleanor Heyward could serve as a study in stress. The fifty-three-year-old daughter is, in her own words, "being driven out of my mind by the mother from hell." The words seem particularly harsh because they are uttered by a soft-seeming woman, someone with the charm and easy manner to quickly make a friend of an acquaintance. But Eleanor, an only child, is steely in describing the woman who brought her into this world and then behaved as if that's where her responsibility began and ended.

"My mother cares only about herself; the whole world revolves around her," says Eleanor. "That's how she's always been and, at eighty-three, that's the way she still is, only more so. Mom is a hypochondriac who has taken medication her whole life. To her, every headache is a brain tumor; an attack of arthritis is lupus."

Tired of having to make frequent three-hour trips to her mother's home in order to check out the latest complaints,

Eleanor decided that her life would be easier if her mother lived closer, so two years ago she found a place near her own home for the older woman. If anything, the move has made life more difficult for the daughter. "I see my mother almost every day," she says, "because she demands it. She claims that she is dying, and when I get there it turns out that she wants me to take her shopping. Or go to lunch with her. Or she needs to see a doctor for a routine checkup, which is something she ought to be able to handle herself.

"This should be the time when my husband and I can enjoy life," Eleanor says, "yet I'm fragmented in my work, I don't get to see friends anymore, and I can't remember the last time I managed to see a movie or read a book."

Resolving the Relationship

It's not unusual to find people like Eleanor among the caregiving population: sons and daughters who go the extra mile in caring for an older parent out of a wish for recognition and, perhaps, reconciliation—their final chance to create some longed-for closeness. For here is what Eleanor also says, "I thought that by having my mother move closer, having her near me, she and I would come to an understanding. I've tried to relate to her. I tried to get her to relate to me. She doesn't care or listen. It's no use. I can't talk to my mother, never could. . . ."

Beatrice, a woman who visits her ailing mother daily, who brushes the older woman's long gray hair and reads her stories from a Chinese-language paper, explains, "What I'm doing for my mother now is what I wish she had done for me."

The desire to right past wrongs is strong. Many men and women find that during this period of life, when they may have more time to spend with their parents, they do manage to work out some of the issues that lie between them. Says Anna Zimmer of The Brookdale Center on Aging, "They may rake up the old garbage, but they do resolve some things. It may not be in the ideal way they would have liked, but at least stuff gets out in the open. It is an opportunity."

Others, like Eleanor, find that reconciliation eludes them, and that the desire for reconciliation, the pressure to resolve issues, becomes yet another burden of caregiving. Grown children have to accept that if love, caring, and respect haven't been given them by the parent all along, it is unlikely that they will receive that appreciation now.

Dealing with your feelings is not easy, but it is important for adult children to make the effort to resolve past conflicts with their parents—to confront hurts and resentments and lay them to rest—in order to reduce the stress of caregiving. Gerontologist Rose Dobrof advises, "Seek help if need be, through friends, family, support groups. If there are serious rifts, consider using a counselor or family therapist to help you come to terms with your parents for your own benefit, if not for theirs. The grief involved when parents die can be less complicated and prolonged if honest attempts are made to resolve them when your parents are alive."

Caregiver Gillian Adams speaks to the value of resolving the relationship with your parent. The fifty-year-old writer, who lives with her husband and three children in San Antonio, was the only child of parents who were married for fourteen years before she entered their lives. "I grew up feeling like I was stuck in a house that I didn't belong in, and that nobody in it particularly wanted me," she says.

"My father was loving but distant. My mother was someone with whom I had had a difficult relationship all of my life. She had always been critical of me. If I got straight A's, she would say, 'You weren't elected May Queen.' If I wrote a book, she would say, 'Why didn't you write *Gone With the Wind?* No matter what I did, she could always come up with something to put me down. So I had a lot of resentment and anger and hostility toward my mother. But when she became widowed and ill, I found that I had other feelings, as well. Part of me hated her, part of me loved her, and part of me, as the only child, felt terribly responsible.

"When she began to fail, Mother refused to leave Mississippi, where she was born and bred, insisting also on remaining in her own home. I hired home-care workers (in the South, they're called 'sitters') to be with my mother. I would also visit her about five times a year, each time staying for a week. (I had two children at home at the time, and had to make elaborate plans for their care during my absence.)

"On one visit, I noticed a gash on my mother's leg. She said that she had fallen. The sitters told me that she'd fallen a few times. We got her a walker, but she wouldn't use it. Before Christmas, Mother fell and broke her hip. In her terms, it was 'the beginning of the end.' And I guess it was. The crisis calls to my home increased—'Her blood count is down; she seems to have an infection'—and I'd leave my family and go running. It was very stressful."

More stressful, Gillian found, was the realization that there were many things that needed to be resolved in her relationship with her mother . . . and that time was running out. She went to see a therapist. "In therapy, I did a lot of work on my mother's family, and I was able to piece together her life and her emotional constipation. I could see my mother as someone who started out as a beautiful young spirit, and who was squashed, first by her family, and later by my father. I could see her as someone who was *unable* to give me what I wanted from her.

"Suddenly, I could look at this poor woman who was lying there and think, *Oh my God, this is just so sad. And I feel so sorry for her.* And I was able to sit there and hold her hand and talk to her for hours, and tell her all these things, tell her that I knew we had never gotten along but that now I understood that what I had resented were things that she could not share. We were coming from two different places, she and I, yet now here we were together—mother and daughter. And I could forgive her.

"I was also asking her forgiveness of me for being what she perceived as this little inquisitive thing who was forever nattering at her, demanding more. I don't know if my mother understood anything I said to her in those last weeks and months of her life, but I like to think that she did. I was very, very pleased that I was able to work it out on the scene, as it were, because if I hadn't, I would have been in very bad shape and unable to care for my mother, which would only have increased the pain and guilt. I was very grateful."

A 1993 poll conducted by the Gallup organization for *Health* magazine asked this question: Which of the following situations do you fear most when you think about your parents getting older? The second most popular response (immediately following the fear that a parent will be forced to live in a nursing home) was: My parents will die suddenly without my having had the chance to say good-bye.

The period of caregiving presents sons and daughters with the opportunity to grow closer to a parent, to resolve differences (if possible), and to say good-bye in a way that rounds out the relationship.

Maintaining a Sense of Perspective

In *Seven Steps to Effective Parent Care,* Donna Cohen and Carl Eisdorfer write, "The important lesson [for caregivers] is to try to place the past and your feelings about the past into perspective and deal with specific tasks that will lead to a responsible level of care for your parent's well-being."

Being old or ill does not give the patient the right to abuse the caregiver. Grown sons and daughters, along with other relatives involved in caring for the older parent, have got to learn how not to play into a parent's manipulations, as Eleanor does when she responds to all of her mother's demands, but to set limits—gently, if at all possible, but in any case firmly.

I learned an important lesson in staying afloat from Augusta Jacobs, whom I met while attending an informational program for caregivers at a local community center. During the question-and-answer period, I discovered that Augusta is involved in the care of her mother-in-law, an eighty-six-year-old woman whom the daughter-in-law describes as being "bright, beautiful, and highly demanding." I was impressed by the equanimity that Augusta seems to bring to her duties, and I asked if I could call on her later, to learn how she copes. She agreed to a meeting.

Augusta, who is fifty-nine, runs a small advertising agency

with her husband, Ira; together they have five children, three of whom are married. Ira's mother, Sophie, needs constant help. Says Augusta, "She's very forgetful, often incontinent, has arthritis, has fallen." Sophie lives in her own apartment, where she's cared for by two women, working day and night shifts. She comes to stay with her son and daughter-in-law every weekend, from Friday afternoon through Sunday.

"We thought it would be better this way," says Augusta. "For one thing, it gives the women who care for my mother-in-law a rest. For another, this is a lively household. My children come by, and their friends, and she does enjoy that. But if they fail to greet her right away, she won't talk to them for the rest of the day."

Like Eleanor Heyward's mother, Augusta's mother-in-law is a woman who demands constant attention. The increased self-absorption of certain older persons is understandable, as they see their horizons limited and their role in the world reduced by age and infirmity. Still, such self-centeredness can (and often does) become rankling. Augusta says about her mother-in-law Sophie, "She always needs to be told how beautiful she is. If you talk about something, she will ask, 'What has that to do with me?'" Then Augusta laughs. "It's funny after a while," she says.

Over the years, Augusta tells me, she has developed a list of guidelines that have enabled her to cope with the demands of caring for a very difficult woman. She shares them:

Make time for yourself. "During the summer," says Augusta, "since I no longer have my weekends free, I take Tuesdays off from work and go to the beach with a friend."

Find a hobby. "I recently took up painting and attend

class every Monday night. I'm not very good at it, but I enjoy it. I lose myself completely. It's important to find something that takes you away from everything. Other people may go swimming or bowling. . . . Just find something for yourself."

Find a support group when you need it. "I joined a six-week workshop for caregivers. Everybody told of their own issues. Solutions came just from talking and listening to other people, to how they were handling things. I'd come home and think, *Thank God, I'm handling things pretty well.* I got a lot out of it."

Don't expect anything. "Sundays, for example, I always used to enjoy going places—antique shows, auctions, arts and crafts exhibits. I can't do that anymore, so I decided: don't *expect* to do it. If you expect something, and it doesn't work out, you get very frustrated. If there's something really special that you want to do, ask someone to come by and help out. Basically, it's best to accept things as they are. I'm not frustrated on Sundays anymore. I used to be. It took me at least a year to make the adjustment. Now I know, 'This is what I do,' and I'm okay with it."

Don't make things look too easy. "I had an aunt whom I used to take care of. She had a stroke, and I would do her shopping, pay the bills, oversee the women who took care of her. In the beginning, other family members would help out with the chores, and would visit her more often. Because I seemed to be managing so smoothly, people stopped asking if I needed help. Eventually, I found that everything was on my head, and I resented it. From that I learned that you have to ask for help. Even if you *can* do it all, there's no reason why you have to."

Never try to do two things at once. "This is something

that has been very helpful to me. If I was helping my mother-in-law shower or dress, I would try to run out and do something in the kitchen. Invariably, my mother-in-law would sense that she was taking my time . . . or something would break in the kitchen. I'd get very frazzled, and so would she. So I learned: if you're going to do something for your parent, just focus your attention on the task at hand and let everything else go. It works."

Go slow. It will save time and effort in the long run. "When caring for a frail older person, accept that things just take longer. If we have to be out of the house at twelve-thirty, I start getting my mother-in-law ready at eleven-thirty. If you want something done right away, forget it. Give each task the time it needs."

Make answers simple and direct. "A question like 'Where should I sit?' requires the answer 'Sit here' instead of 'Sit anywhere you want.' You may want to give the older person a choice, but listen to the question. They may want direction."

Learn the parent's habits, and try to accommodate them. "We used to leave our toothbrushes in the bathroom, but we found that my mother-in-law would use all our toothbrushes. So now we put ours away, and leave only one toothbrush out: hers. Sophie sometimes will use towels for things other than drying her hands. So now we keep our towels in our bedrooms, and I throw hers in the wash frequently."

By keeping her mother-in-law's needs in focus, and her own as well, Augusta Jacobs is able to manage the difficult tasks of caregiving with seeming ease. It is an ease that results as much from deliberation as dedication.

Drawing the Line: Setting Limits

People have different abilities and thresholds of stress, behaviors that they're able to tolerate and tasks that they're not able to tolerate. Amy Horowitz of the Lighthouse Research Institute advises, "It's important for caregivers to be honest with themselves about what they can and cannot do. And to say to themselves, *It's okay not to do it all.*"

At a given point, every caregiver has to decide, "If A, B, or C happens with my relative, then I will have to seek an alternative plan: hire someone to provide home care, search out a senior residence, begin to investigate nursing homes."

Geriatric care manager Nick Newcombe says, "The most important thing to help people with caregiving is to get them to understand why they are doing it, what the patient's needs are versus what their own needs are, and where they must draw the line. Otherwise, they will drown.

"But the line is different for different people," Newcombe continues. "Some people draw the line at fecal incontinence, others at mental incapacity. Some begin looking at nursing homes when their parent has difficulty negotiating the stairs to the attic. No guidebook can tell you how much care is needed, what your role should be, and when it's time to relinquish the care of a parent to others. Only you can determine that, and the way to reach that determination is by keeping the focus clear: understanding the needs of the patient and knowing just what you are willing and able to do in response, then turning to others to accomplish what else is needed.

"Keep in mind that the line is not etched in stone," he says. "It is a projected goal. Some people reach their line and find that they can do more; others wear out before they reach a previously defined line. They have to alter their plans."

The point is that most caregivers have not made any decisions about what they're going to do "in case." They drift along, feeling befuddled, inadequate, or overwhelmed. Drawing a line helps introduce an air of reality and sense of purpose to the tasks at hand. It opens the door to asking for help from others, and accepting assistance, if and when it is needed.

To summarize, adult sons and daughters who become involved in caregiving will find the process eased if they:

- are clear about their reasons for involvement—why they are engaged, what they hope to accomplish;
- accept the fact that they cannot do it all;
- set (flexible) limits as to the extent of their commitment;
- request cooperation from family members as needed or desired;
- seek support from friends and groups;
- pay attention to their own needs as well as the needs of the parent;
- work on ways to resolve a distant or destructive relationship with a parent, for the caregiver's own sake and well-being.

A knowledge of the parent's needs and a realistic assessment of one's own ability to meet those needs sometimes leads caregivers to make difficult decisions, the toughest of which is a decision to consider nursing home placement. That action, and the steps leading to it, are taken up in the next chapter.

CHAPTER 10

THE NURSING HOME DECISION

As a child of nine or ten adventuring to the outer ranges of my neighborhood, I would sometimes find myself heading past a high stone wall, topped by wire and bits of broken glass, that surrounded a large brick building set on grounds extending the length and width of a full city block. It was a reformatory, a place where children were sent when they were bad and, if local lore was true, from which they could not escape. I never saw or heard any of the children in residence, for whenever I was in the area I would walk rapidly and purposefully past the structure, barely sneaking a glance within, the sooner to put it behind me.

In much the same manner, and with a similar sense of foreboding, I have since found myself hurrying past nursing homes, the bogeymen of our middle and later years. As in the past, I have felt the urgent need to place distance between myself and the institution. The warning that sounds in my mind at such times is the same one I heard when going by the reformatory: *This is a place to be avoided at all costs.*

It hasn't helped that, over the years, my mother periodically has said to me, "God forbid that I should end up in a home." I always echoed her sentiment, "God forbid." This exchange (or some variation thereof) will no doubt sound familiar to many readers. We do not want our parents to end up in a home if we can help it. They do not want to be there.

It is not always possible or advisable, however, for the disabled elderly to continue to reside in their own homes or to be cared for in the home of a child or other family member. There are times when the condition of the patient or the situation of the caregiver make relocating a parent to an eldercare facility the only sensible decision. Often, of course, there *is* no decision to be made. A medical emergency, such as a stroke, requires hospitalization, after which a patient is transferred to a skilled nursing facility. The decision is pretty much taken out of the family's hands.

Accepting the move is a different story. In the eyes of the son or daughter, allowing a parent to move into a nursing home is likely to be viewed as abandonment, as warehousing, as the ultimate failure. The emotional landscape is bleak.

If you are not yet there, not yet at the point of placement, it's a likely assumption that the thought of residential care for your parent may have entered your mind at some time—perhaps on a day when you receive a long-distance phone call from your mother or father indicating that there is a problem, only you're not there to handle it. Or on a day when the current home-care aide fails to show up. Or on a day, for example, when you feel stretched to the limit, unable to manage the needs of the older person and still meet the demands of your job or find time for your spouse or your children or yourself. On the kind of day that every caregiver comes up against once in a while, the words "look into a home" may cross your mind.

More than likely, you'll dismiss them at first: *no, never, not for my mother or father.* Then there will be another crisis, perhaps several bad days stretching into a week or two of feeling overwhelmed by your parent's needs and your own inability to adequately meet them, and the thought of a home will come to the fore once again.

When Is the Parent Ready?

"The most frequently asked question that comes up when we talk about nursing home placement is, 'When is the parent ready?'" says Gail Hoffmann, volunteer coordinator at the Alzheimer's Association's New York City chapter. And the answer? "The parent is *never* ready for a nursing home," she says. "The right time is determined by when the *caregiver* is ready."

Helaine Gross knows the truth of that statement. A devoted daughter, she struggled to maintain her mother and father, both of them infirm and ailing, in their own home long after she knew, intellectually, that a different plan was needed. Emotionally, she did not want to accept their decline even though it was patently clear that her parents, both in their late eighties, could no longer manage on their own or even with hired help.

Looking back, Helaine says, "I could see two types of problems. My father's mind was beginning to go. He'd be visiting us, for example, and I would come upon him in the garage. He was looking for his car, he said, when he hadn't owned a car or driven one for several years. Or we'd be visiting my daughter, and he'd be up and dressed at one in the morning because he had a meeting to attend.

"We finally realized that my mother had been covering up for Dad, and she was exhausted. She had coped magnificently for a long time . . . too long. She was failing physically, while my father was failing mentally. And I was making the one-hour trip to their home several times a week, trying to meet the needs of both. Then I'd drive home (another hour's ride, this time in rush-hour traffic) to have dinner with my husband, after which I'd work until one or two in the morning in order to meet job deadlines.

"During this time, I'd been experiencing terrible pain in my jaw. My dentist referred me to an endodontist, who examined my mouth and then told me, 'You don't need root canal; you need yoga.' It turns out that I had been clenching my teeth and I wasn't even aware of it. That's when I realized that my stress level was very high and that I had to do something about it. The next day, I did two things: I joined a square dance group and I began to make inquiries about residential facilities."

Helaine discovered a wide range of elder-care facilities, many of them a far cry from the colorless and confining places that so many of us envision when the words "nursing home" are uttered. When looking for a facility for your parents, it's important to determine the level of care needed. What her parents needed, Helaine decided, was an assisted living community for her mother, and a dementia unit or skilled nursing facility for her father.

There are about 65,000 assisted living projects across the nation, offering residents twenty-four-hour supervision, meals, transportation, medication management, help with dressing and grooming, and recreational programs. Limited health and nursing care is provided, however. When such care is needed, residents (or their families) often have to hire home attendants or private nurses to provide it, or arrange for the parent to be moved to a skilled nursing facility where more intensive care is available.

Helaine's parents now live in a health-care complex that is located within a fifteen-minute drive of her own home. (**What helps:** Having a parent move to a home that is easily accessible and convenient is one way to ease the burden on the caregiver.) It comprises an independent living facility, where her mother resides; a dementia facility, where her father stayed for two weeks until it was determined that he needed more care; and a nursing unit, his current home. He is visited there daily by his wife; Helaine sees her parents at least once a week. "For their own sake and for mine," she says, "the move to a home should have been made earlier."

Readiness, of course, is defined differently by each caregiver (and by each parent, if the older person is capable of being involved in the decision). Certain provocations, however, commonly lead adult children to consider nursing home care for their parents. According to Rose Dobrof, executive director of The Brookdale Center on Aging, the most stressful situations involve loss of sleep, incontinence, and bizarre behavior.

"Let's look at loss of sleep," she explains. "Take the typical situation where the parent doesn't live with the child. What happens is that the old person is not sleeping well at night, is wakeful and living alone, and will call the child at all hours of the night." Dr. Dobrof, who was formerly assistant director of The Hebrew Home for the Aged in Riverdale, New York, says, "Time and again at the Home, we would see that the straw that broke the camel's back, leading children to seek placement for the parent, was when the night calls were constant."

Caregiver Richard Lauffer (whom we met in chapter 6) would be phoned half a dozen times a day by his mother, an Alzheimer's sufferer for whom day and night had become indistinguishable. At night, the telephone in the son's house would ring just as often, jarring the whole family awake. Parents and children were left with jangled nerves that had them on edge throughout the following day. Clearly, something had to be done.

"At first, I'd try leaving the answering machine on at night," says Richard, "although that didn't stop the ringing; it only cut it off earlier. My next solution was to take the receiver off the hook when the family went to sleep, but then I'd lie in bed worrying, *What if there really is an emergency?* So I would get up, tiptoe over to the phone, and replace the receiver. Instantly, the ringing would resume." Although loss of sleep was not the only reason for Richard's decision, finally, to seek a nursing home for his mother, who had also taken to wandering, certainly it was a contributing factor.

There are different solutions, of course. Other families, faced with the same provocation, have responded by hiring "sleepover help" to be with the disoriented parent through the night, thus addressing both the nuisance and safety concerns. The decision to place a parent, as Richard Lauffer acknowledges, is based on not one but a variety of considerations.

Incontinence, another factor listed by Rose Dobrof, is very difficult for families to face. The gerontologist notes, "I always used to say that God didn't intend for daughters or sons to toilet their parents." Of course, some children have no problem in dealing with incontinence, but many do.

She continues, "Bizarre behavior, the third factor, involves several things—like not being able to take the parent out anywhere for fear of their behavior. There's also the matter of what has been called 'the loss of self.' That is, you're taking care of somebody who isn't the person that he or she was. Further, the parent doesn't recognize the child, or gets the generations mixed up, which can be very disturbing." When the person you love is progressively deteriorating, and other care options have been exhausted (home-care workers come and go; day care is no longer appropriate; medications, changed frequently, have become ineffective), a nursing home can begin to seem like the best alternative.

Long-distance caregiving, where it becomes difficult for the son or daughter to oversee the parent's condition and to assess the care plan that has been put in place, is a fourth factor leading children to consider residential placement.

Yet another concern for caregivers is the isolation of the disabled parent, which results from a number of causes. For one thing, so many of the older person's contemporaries— spouses, sisters and brothers, lifelong friends—are no longer alive to provide social and emotional support. For another, remaining friends and family often drift away from the person who suffers from stroke, Parkinson's, dementia, or some other devitalizing ailment. They don't want to witness the debilitation, or they're unwilling to make the effort to communicate with someone who must struggle to respond. Isolation is compounded when a parent and child live at a distance from one another. The result is that the older person is left virtually alone, perhaps dependent on one care attendant. For such patients, nursing homes can offer socialization—people who talk to you, people to eat with.

There is also the factor of cost. Although home care is generally less expensive than institutional care, there are times when a patient reaches the point where two or more people are needed to provide care, physical therapy, or other special services. Sometimes it takes two people just to lift a patient from his bed to the wheelchair. Not only are such multiple services expensive, they can often be better provided in a nursing home with skilled aides.

Locating a Home: The Search

For any of a number of reasons, then, the caregiver may reach a point where it makes sense, at the very least, to begin to gather information about senior residences: what's available, what's required to gain entry. *It won't hurt to do some research into the subject,* you tell yourself, although you also tell yourself you don't plan to act on what you find. If you're like me, you go to the library first, seek out books on how to select a nursing home, and discover that there are many. You browse through them.

All the guidebooks offer this same advice: the best time to

begin looking for a nursing home is before it is necessary. All recommend that you visit several homes to find "the right one for your parent."

The local office of the Department of Aging is a good place to begin your search. They will supply you with a list of homes in your area. Another place to contact is the National Citizens Coalition for Nursing Home Reform, 1424 16th Street, NW, Suite 202, Washington, DC 20036 (tel: [202] 332-2275), for information on ombudsman and consumer groups in your area, to help answer a specific question, or to help you solve a problem. Asking doctors and friends for their recommendations or consulting with a geriatric care manager or elder-law attorney can also be useful.

The Visit

If you decide to embark on a preliminary investigation of available facilities, you may find yourself visiting an elder-care establishment, as my husband Noel and I did a while ago on a weekday afternoon. We were there to see if this was a viable option for my mother-in-law, who lives in her own home and is cared for by a devoted aide.

A once gregarious woman renowned for her storytelling and wit, my mother-in-law had become isolated by age and infirmity. Mom might do better in a congregate living facility where she could meet with other elderly people, her daughter thought, and asked us to see this place. Noel called ahead and made an appointment.

We entered the building, a high-rise that was in the process of being converted from a transient hotel to an independent living residence. The doorman was courteous, the lobby abandoned. It was lunchtime, explained a young woman who arrived to take us on a tour of the facility.

Escorting us through a series of small, interconnecting rooms off the lobby, she explained that these areas were being used temporarily as dining rooms while a larger and brighter communal dining area was being constructed. The day's menu, posted at the entrance, offered a choice of hamburger or chicken. A fair number of the white-haired residents were already seated at lunch, many of them in wheelchairs, others with walkers drawn close to the table. Quite a few of the diners were being assisted by private attendants who, we later learned, were not part of the staff but were independently hired by the residents or their families. We saw no interaction among the residents. Everyone ate at separate tables, silently.

Next we were led through an alcove where a recreational therapist stood at a low folding table. She was cutting out pieces of cardboard in preparation for the afternoon's activity: making paper dolls. It was an arts and crafts project that a kindergartner might disdain. "Sometimes," said our guide, "we have entertainment for the residents. Yesterday evening, we played bingo."

"We can't have Mom come to live here," I said fiercely, seeing in my mind's eye the once-vibrant woman who even now deserved better. Noel agreed. We left the building, dejected. And this was a luxury residence for men and women who were more or less able to navigate on their own or with some assistance! It was not a nursing home.

We also wondered whether, had we found the place inviting, we would have been able to afford to have Mom stay there. We looked at the figures that had been provided for us, did some quick calculation, and were astounded by the cost of room, board, and basic care. One could rent a villa on the Riviera for less. It was clear that we had much to learn.

And so do we all.

What to Look for When You Visit

The more information you gather, the more secure you will feel if and when a decision is made for placement. It is not unusual for caregivers to look at a half dozen or more sites in the process. Each visit provides answers and inspires new questions. In the long run, I assure you, all of that is helpful.

When planning to visit a nursing home, it's a good idea to ask someone to accompany you. This is a highly emotional experience, and you can use the support of a friend. You will also benefit from having a second pair of eyes available, for there is much to be seen and considered.

Some points to keep in mind:

• When you enter the building, does it seem pleasant? Does it give you an institutional or a homey feeling?

• Ask to see residents' rooms. Do the quarters appear cheerful or depressing? Is there a uniformity about them or are they enhanced by personal belongings? Are photos and mementos on display? Is there enough drawer and closet space? Some elder-care establishments encourage residents to bring their own furniture—bed, dresser, reading lamp; others are willing to make space for a favorite chair or an afghan, but many homes are less accommodating. You will want to consider this.

• Is there an odor of urine or a strong antiseptic smell? Accidents will happen, but a well-maintained home does not have an odor.

• Are bathrooms private or communal? Have they been outfitted with safety features, such as grab bars and rails?

• Ask whether there's an outdoor recreation area. Do residents use it?

• Request a schedule of activities. Check to see that the activity listed for the time of your visit is, in fact, taking place, and that people are involved and interested.

• As you walk through the home, you will, of course, observe the residents. Are most ambulatory or are they confined to wheelchairs? In some homes, policy requires the use of wheelchairs (even when they aren't needed by residents) as a means of ensuring against falls, a frequent problem for the aged. This can be significant if your parent is able to get around on his own or with the use of a walker, and you don't want him or her to become dependent on a wheelchair.

• Are residents wearing house dresses and bathrobes— do they walk around in hospital garb or are they dressed in their own daytime outfits to help them maintain pride and self-identity?

• If you can comfortably speak to some of the residents, do so. Ask about the day's menu or about a recent activity. You can learn much from their evaluations.

• On your tour, don't fail to pay attention to the manner in which staff members interact with residents. Are they warm? Courteous? Do they address people by name—as Mrs. Jones or Bessie—or do they employ the impersonal "honey" or "dear"? Do they talk down to patients or, worse, ignore them? (In one home I visited, I was struck by a scene in which two elderly people were each being assisted with eating. Their aides carried on a conversation with one another, spoon-feeding the patients but otherwise ignoring the women in their care.)

• Try to have visits coincide with lunch or dinner hours. Check to see if there's a menu and if residents are offered a choice of dishes. Do they seem to be enjoying their food, finishing their meals? Look at the social atmosphere: do residents sit together? Do they talk to one another? Says Judith Brickman, long-term-care coordinator with the New York City Department for the Aging, "If the home doesn't let you come when there's a meal, if you're told, 'Sorry, we don't like to have our residents disturbed at mealtime,' look elsewhere."

What to Ask

Your first visits to a home can be so disconcerting that you're unlikely to remember all that you intended to ask or all the answers you are given. It is helpful, therefore, to come prepared with a list of questions, and to jot down pertinent replies.

• You will want to know about licensing and staffing. What organization accredits the home? Is a qualified physician always on call? Are rehabilitation therapists on staff? How many, and how are they used? Is there competent and concerned round-the-clock nursing? What is the ratio of nurses to aides? To patients? Is staff training provided on a regular basis?

• Are there liberal visiting hours? This shows recognition of patients' social and emotional needs and also that the home is not trying to hide something.

• If the residence has different levels of care, as is the case with the complex that Helaine Gross found for her parents, how are decisions for transfer made, and will the caregiver be consulted about any changes?

• Are family members informed of, and invited to attend, conferences to discuss the progress of the patient and the appropriateness of the care plan?

• Is there a residents' council or other means of involving patients in their own welfare?

• If the patient requires hospitalization, will the room be held for his or her return . . . and for how long?

• Are residents permitted to leave the home for periods of time (to visit a family member, for example) and for how long?

• Are social workers available to patients and families?

• Are there support groups run by the institution?

• If appropriate, can husband and wife room together? (You may recall that this was an important issue for Laura Wolensky, whom we met in chapter 6. Locating a home that didn't force Laura's mother and father to separate, after so many years of living together, contributed to the parents' adjustment and to this caring daughter's peace of mind.)

• If religious services are important to your parent, ask about their availability. Similarly, ethnic and cultural preferences may be a consideration. One son was dismayed to learn that his mother was the only Spanish-speaking resident of the senior residence he had found for her nearest his home. After he arranged to have his mother relocated to a place where there were others of the same culture, even though it was out of the neighborhood, both the son and his mother felt much happier.

- Does the home cater to special dietary needs? Are ethnically appropriate foods available, if that is a consideration?
- How is personal cash handled? Theft is endemic to most nursing homes and senior residences. You'll want to know the best way to safeguard money and personal belongings, although you will probably be fighting a losing battle.
- Ask about costs—not just how much, but what is included in the basic fee. Families are often surprised to find themselves billed for everything from Band-Aids to diapers, from doctors' examinations to hairdressers' visits—charges over and above the cost of room and board. You will want some idea of what you may expect.
- Will the home accept Medicare or Medicaid payments? Members of the nursing home staff can be very helpful in arranging for a resident to become eligible for Medicaid. The availability of social workers in hospitals and nursing homes has become fairly common. It's useful to keep in mind that these able professionals have far more experience in dealing with the tangles of regulations governing placement and payment than you do. They also help families cope with their anxiety and grief. Allow them to hold your hand through the process: *you don't have to take this walk alone.*

Enlisting siblings or other significant family members in decision making also can help to lighten the burden. Keep in mind, however, that your brothers or sisters may see things differently than you do, especially if you're the more committed caregiver and they live at a distance and visit the parent infrequently. They may, for example, be freer in advocating increased home care instead of placing the parent in a nursing home when you've been heavily involved in providing that care . . . and are ready to jump out the window.

When family members disagree on how best to manage parent care, it can be useful to enlist the aid of a qualified third party in making the nursing home decision. The parent's physician, the hospital social worker (in cases where the parent is being moved from a hospital), a trusted member of the clergy, or a skilled geriatric care counselor may all be appropriate choices.

Finally, trust your instincts. After you have visited several residences, large and small, you will begin to get a feeling for the kind of place that might best suit your parent's needs and meet your own requirements. You may now be ready to make application and start in motion the various procedures and assessments that are necessary in order for your parent to qualify for placement. (Criteria for nursing home admission differ from state to state; depending on where your parent lives, you may find that you're required to have the assessment procedure completed before you can make application to a nursing home.)

Introducing the Idea to Your Parent

While it's generally not a good idea for the caregiver to include a parent in the initial search (if these visits are upsetting to the adult son or daughter, think how much more traumatic they can be for the prospective patient), you now may be ready to involve your parent. There is no easy, one-size-fits-all way to go about this. The method you use depends a lot on your knowledge of your parent, how best to approach him or her, and the condition of the parent: how much he or she is able to be involved.

One caregiver introduced the idea of making the move by bringing her mother brochures and photographs of the place she favored and sharing what she liked about it. Another daughter looked at about a dozen different senior homes, then took her mother to visit the two she liked best. "Mom selected the one that I would have chosen," says the daughter, who felt pleased that the ultimate decision was her mother's.

Not every parent is so accommodating. Some will not be willing to listen when the idea of making the move to a nursing home is raised. "The subject was anathema to my mother," says caregiver Nora Sheppard, "yet my brother and I had finally reached a point where we saw no other way to meet Mom's considerable and growing needs. Neither of us could provide the personal and daily care she required, nor could we afford to hire competent round-the-clock help or a geriatric care service that could function in our stead."

The promise to Mom that "I'm never going to put you in a nursing home" is a promise that the caregiver may not be able to keep. Nora was concerned that her mother would fall one more time, would someday suffer one more stroke, and that the decision about her care would be taken out of the family's hands. "I had recurrent nightmares about Mother entering the county home," she says. "I knew I had to do something to try to keep that from happening."

In desperation one day, Nora placed a phone call to a

Quaker home that she had heard about (ironically, from her mother, who had once visited a friend there). A former estate, it had been redesigned as a home for the elderly and infirm. "Bring your mother in," she was told, "and we'll see if she meets our requirements."

"My mother did not want to go," Nora says, "but my brother Gabe and I were insistent. Together with Mom, we drove out to see the home. It was a silent ride, with each of us deep in thoughts of the unspeakable, and . . ." Nora says, her voice turning bright at the memory, "it turned out to be a magical day.

"For some reason my mother and the home's director hit it off, and there was such good feeling in the room," she continues. "In the beginning of the interview, the director had pointed at her desk and said, 'I have five drawers filled with applications.' I remember thinking, *We don't have time for years to elapse before Mother can come to live here.* Then, at some later point in the interview, the director asked my mother what her income was, and Mother told her the amount—it was very low—and defiantly added, 'I earned every penny of it.' The director got up from her desk, walked over to Mother, shook her hand, and said, 'And I earned all of mine, too.'

"The next thing she told my mother was, 'There's a room across the way. Would you like it?' My brother's heart and mine were in our mouths because our mother had been so set against moving to a home, but Mother simply said, 'Yes.'

"The second miracle was that we were able to work out the financial arrangements. It was very expensive. It was like being at a resort on a regular basis. We were asked how much we could afford. Gabe and I each agreed to contribute a specific amount of money monthly, supplementing our mother's social security payments, which would now go to the home. Further, we learned that the home had an annuity that enabled them to provide a kind of scholarship to deserving elders who would otherwise be unable to meet the regular monthly costs. My mother would qualify for this assistance.

"Everything seemed to be falling into place," Nora says, "and then Mother failed the mental exam by three points! This meant that she could not be admitted to the room in the independent living section of the home, but would have to be placed on a waiting list for admission to the personal care wing. It could take fourteen months for a bed in that wing to become available, the director said."

Waiting: What You Can Do to Make It Easier

When the parent's name is placed on a waiting list, there are steps that the caregiving child can take to (perhaps) speed the process. One expert recommends to caregivers that they practice the art of "creative nudging," which she defines as: a phone call placed to the office of admissions, every ten days or so, just to inquire if your parent has moved up on the list and to remind them of your interest. "That's not overdoing it," she says.

While waiting for a room to become available for her mother, Nora wrote and rewrote a letter to the director of the home, thanking her for her courtesy and efforts to help the family. Nora also shared her very genuine fear that, if a space did not soon become available at the Quaker residence, her mother would have to be placed in the county nursing home. It was a candid account of the situation and Nora's feelings. Within six months of mailing the letter, Nora received notice that a place had become available in the personal care wing. Her mother could move in right away.

"The next day," says Nora, "my brother Gabe and I moved some of Mother's furniture into her new room, and helped her get settled. As we left the residence that afternoon, Gabe turned to me and said, 'Nora, we just handed over the baton.' We walked out on a cloud, and I've been there ever since.

"I still call and see Mother frequently," Nora continues. "I generally try to time my visits so that I can have lunch with her. The residence has a beautiful dining room—chandeliered and clean, in sharp and welcome contrast to the dingy room that my mother's kitchen had become over the years of her decline. When I used to visit my mother at home, I would cringe when I needed to open the cabinets. I would find myself washing each and every plate and saucer before I used it. At the nursing home, we are served with linen napkins.

"I also feel at peace knowing that help is available whenever Mother needs it. Once when I was on vacation, I phoned her and there was no answer, so I called the nurse, who told me that my mother had broken her hip. I was upset, but this could have happened to her at home—indeed, it *had* happened before. The difference was that this time there were people around to pick her up and to see that she received timely and appropriate medical care. Still, I cut my vacation short and came running. Because that's what daughters do."

How to Work with the Nursing Home

The role of the caregiving child does not end when a parent enters a home, it changes. While you may have handed over the baton, you're still a leading member of the orchestra. Contrary to popular belief, there's no rule that states you have to play a dirge. I don't want to minimize the effects of placement on the caregiver, who at this time is confronted with a range of conflicting emotions.

Barbara Miller, a caring daughter, describes them well: "When my mother moved out of her home and into a nursing home closer to me, I was really happy because now I'd be able to see her more often, but I was terribly sad because I knew that she would never go back to her own home. I cried my eyes out. I tell you, I don't think any of these are good decisions. I think they are choices, and I think this was the right choice."

But that's what caring for the caregiver is about, isn't it? Making responsible choices. As Barbara also says, "Part of taking care of myself was to arrange for my mother to move into a senior-care facility instead of taking her into my home and hiring nursing help."

She adds, "Sometimes, when I have felt guilty about the decision, I would make myself remember how much my mother had valued her own independence, and I'd know that she would have wanted independence for me."

Being active, assisting the parent to settle into the new surroundings, is a positive act. "I tried to make the move as least disruptive as possible," says Barbara. "On the morning of the appointed day, a moving van arrived to pick up the designated pieces of furniture and drive them to Mother's new quarters in Pleasant Valley Manor—that's not the real name of the home, but it's close enough. My sister flew in so that we could do this together, and we drove our mother toward her new residence. Along the way, we stopped for lunch. Mother kept asking, 'Where am I going?' We told her. She said, 'I hope it will be nice.' We said that we hoped so, too. When we reached the home, her furniture was already in place. We unpacked her clothes, set her up, had dinner together, said goodnight, and went home.

"It was helpful to have stayed to make Mother comfortable," says Barbara. "It also proved beneficial to have my sister with me."

In the beginning, it is important to help the parent become acclimated to his or her new surroundings, even as the adult children also struggle to accept the changes. In addition to the sorrow and the sense of defeat, there's also the practical and extremely emotional task of clearing out a parent's home while the parent is still alive.

Here's what helps: not doing both at the same time. Experts advise that you hold onto the house or apartment for a month or two, three if at all possible. This will enable you and your parent to get used to the placement before you deal with other wrenching issues.

But do bring some favorite photographs from your parent's home to grace the new setting, including pictures of your father and mother taken when they were younger. This is done as much to remind the parent of his or her past as to educate the staff to the fact that the person they are dealing with is not just a white-haired frail elder in a wheelchair or someone who is lost in unreality. This elder human being was a bride or groom, a young parent, a college student, a gardener, a musician, a talented seamstress, a person worthy of respect.

It's a good idea, also, to bring a tape recorder along on your visits and play tapes of favorite songs for your parent. Not only is this a pleasant way to pass the time, but it is another means of introducing staff members to the patient's tastes and background. Basically, the more information you give the home about your parent, the better experience a patient will have.

"Feeling that I was an advocate for my parent was very helpful," says Barbara Miller. "Realizing that I could not do it all myself, making sure that Mother was well cared for by others, helped *me* to feel better. When your parent is no longer strong enough or able to speak for herself, you can make sure that the parent is not wet or dirty or hungry or cold or abused. Frequent visits help."

Barbara made it a practice to visit her mother several times a week. "I always dropped in unannounced, so I could see what was going on," she says. "Also, there's no question in my mind that the residents who have family members visit them get better care."

Placing a parent in a nursing home introduces the caregiver to a whole new set of management issues. Within the first few days or weeks of the parent's entering the home, a patient care conference is held. Family members have a right to be included in that conference. It is a right that should be exercised. Caregivers who live at a distance from the nursing home have found it helpful to hire a geriatric care manager to represent them at the conference, and report back on the proceedings. Some adult children have even arranged to participate in the meeting via conference call. There *are* ways of coping with this new culture.

For patients who are able to articulate their ailments, to say where it hurts, nursing homes can be good settings in which to receive appropriate care. For those who are cognitively impaired, the family has to be much more of an observer and an advocate. Is the patient often sleepy when you arrive? You will want to ask about what medications your parent is receiving, and whether dosages have been increased. Do you notice any bedsores? You will want to find out what type of physical activity is provided daily and weekly. Exercise is important to stem the physical and psychological decline of the patient. During visits, caregivers can help a parent walk—to the outdoor recreation area if possible; to the bathroom, if that is an achievable goal. Even having the parent reach for a glass of water instead of having it handed to him can provide necessary movement.

It's a tricky business, being a "nursing home caregiver." Many grown children who find themselves in this strange new world say that it is helpful to turn to the old hands— children of residents who have been there for a while—for support and guidance.

One of the most effective ways for caregivers to help a parent who is in a nursing home is to determine which of the staff members can be enlisted as partners in care. Most nursing homes are understaffed. Even the most well-intentioned aides, nurses, and social workers seldom have time to do more than the basic necessities for residents. (This is becoming ever more the case in the current climate of budget cuts and staff reductions.) After your parent is settled in, if you notice a problem, bring it to the attention of staff members in an appropriate manner. You don't want to alienate the very people whom you must rely on, but you don't want to ignore your parent's needs, either.

It's a good idea to keep a notebook, jotting down some of your observations ("Tuesday—Mom's lunch arrived cold and late; Thursday—she was still in her nightgown when I arrived at 3:00"), and to follow up on them if the situation doesn't improve during future visits. Speak to the charge nurse. Ask if you can phone her once a week to discuss your parent's care, and set a time when such a call would be welcome.

"Look for moments to support the staff, too," advises a caregiving daughter who has made it a point to stop by and see her mother in the home several days a week. "Write a letter to the director of nursing and commend those people who are particularly helpful to your parent. For one thing, it's an important boost to the morale of staff members who are struggling to manage a difficult job. For another, it encourages them to provide better care."

If problems exist and persist, says Judith Brickman, "it helps to know that there are long-term-care ombudsman programs in every state that act as advocates for nursing home patients."

Having said this, it is also important to point out that an institution is not a home, and that our parents are not likely to receive the kind of care and attention that are possible when they are cared for in a private home by family members or by a home-care aide overseen by family members. Caregivers have to make their peace with this.

Previously, we spoke of the need for adult children to draw a line delineating what they can and cannot take on in terms of parent care. When dealing with the nursing home situation, caregivers help themselves when they learn to draw a line between ideal care and responsible attention. In this, the final chapter of a mother or father's life, it is important for their grown children to see to it that the frail elderly parent is, at the very least, cared for and safe. For some adult children and their parents, those requirements are best met in a nursing home setting.

To sum up, caregivers can help themselves manage the decisions and adjustments of placing a parent in a nursing home by doing the following:

- researching the variety of elder care residences that are available, and determining which type best meets the parent's needs;
- becoming informed about what to look for in a nursing home;
- taking a friend along on preliminary fact-finding visits;
- enlisting siblings and other family members in decision making;
- knowing when outside counsel is necessary, and making use of professional helpers;
- considering the residence's location in terms of convenience for the caregiver;
- finding a place where parent and caregiver can be culturally "at home";
- becoming an advocate for the parent, not only for its positive effect on the parent's care but also because

advocacy helps to offset the caregiver's feelings of helplessness;
- joining a support group at the nursing home;
- abandoning the quest for a perfect solution and learning to live with the present and the possible.

The chapter that follows considers the future.

Chapter 11

WHO'LL BE THERE TO CARE FOR ME?

Witnessing our parents growing older, frailer, less alert and more in need of assistance leads us, their sons and daughters, to reflect on the passage of time and to ponder the future, our own future. Suddenly, we understand that life does indeed go by in the blink of an eye.

For wasn't it only yesterday when my mother shared with me her pride in having been selected to perform in a program at the local senior center? Now she's largely given up going to that center because she is tired of having her attempts at friendship rebuffed by the other, more able seniors and because, sometimes, she forgets that it's Monday or Tuesday, and that the center is open.

Wasn't it just the other day that my mother-in-law told me of switching her Philharmonic subscription from Friday evenings to Saturday afternoons because, she explained, "Your father-in-law and I don't get out as much in the evening. You know—" she said with a wink "—we're not as young as we used to be." But my father-in-law has been gone for many years now, and my mother-in-law has not attended a concert in over a decade.

No, we're none of us as young as we used to be.

As we tend to our aging parents, worry about them, feel guilty, feel angry, feel sad—as we do and feel all these things, we also cling to our parents, for we are not ever ready to be orphaned. Losing our parents makes us the older generation.

The signs of time's passage are everywhere about me. When I find myself lately groping for a word or misplacing my eyeglasses, I begin to worry that, like my mother, I may be losing it. Observing my parent's growing infirmity, I see my own old age as all too imminent.

In caring for our parents, we think about how we *will age.*

Paul, whom we met in chapter 8, seems prematurely to be struggling with this question, but life's circumstances have forced him to face certain issues at this time. Paul's mother, you will recall, had long been a mainstay in her son's life until illness made her turn inward, leaving Paul—an only child who is father to an only child—without his accustomed support. Paul's description of the effect this has had on him, which follows, is insightful and eloquent:

"I think part of the reason I went through a period of being angry is that, for the first time in my life, I was made to confront my own mortality. There was my mother, someone I could always turn to, someone who'd always been there for me, who accepted me no matter what, and who was young and fun and all those things. And that's what I am now, for *my* son.

"But my dad is dead, and my mother is not there in that way for me anymore. And I'm not going to be there in that way for my son some day. Your parent's aging and increasing dependence forces you to come face to face with your own future decline, and so you fight that in the parent. Why? Because that's where you're headed. I understand that now in very personal ways. . . . You can see older people on the street, in other families, other places, and you say, 'Well, all right, that's them.' But this is us, *my* parent and me. And I think it's very hard to accept that.

"So what do I see for my own future? I look at my mother's aging as a learning experience. A successful parent-child relationship is a give-and-take relationship. You have to keep that social compact going. If life works out that I someday have to rely on my son for assistance—physical, financial, or logistical—that's okay as long as I can remember to still give him something: give him an ear, a sense that I care about how things are going for him. It's as simple as saying, 'Tell me what you're doing. . . .' I hope I can do that for my son, for both of us."

We think, *If I should need it, who'll be there to care for me?*

Contemplating a time when they may need to be care recipients instead of care givers, different adult children respond to this question in different ways:

• Barbara, aged sixty-five, is married, works part-time, and still manages to spend two or three days of every week visiting her housebound ninety-four-year-old mother. With four grown children of her own, Barbara says, "In caring for my mother, I'm aware all the time that I'm modeling for my kids. If I grow old and need help, God forbid, I *expect* my children to be there for me."

• Phillipa, sixty and an only child who has been deeply caught up in parent care, is less certain of the future. She says, "If I, who adored my parents, could now feel the way I do toward them as people (not really wanting to be with them, noting that the dishes in their home are chipped, that everything is so shabby), I think: *How is my daughter going to regard me?* She was never as close to me as I was to my parents. She will not be so caring."

• Burton, in his mid-fifties, is far less involved in tending to the needs of his mother and father, both of whom are in their eighties, although he acknowledges that his father's diabetic condition is serious and that his mother, always an able woman, seems increasingly hard put to cope with her husband's declining state. There is an edge to Burton's voice as he declares, "The fact is that I have a responsibility to live my own life. I really believe that. When I grow older, I don't expect my children to be there for me."

• Laura, who is thirty-seven and single, keeps a framed photograph of a silver-haired man on her desk. "That's my dad," she proudly tells visitors to her office. Two years ago, Laura lost her mother. "I can't bear to consider a future without my dad," she says. "If he dies, I won't be anybody's child. I'll finally be grown-up, without ties. And who'll be there to care for me?" Recently, Laura placed an ad in a personals column. "Up to now, I've really enjoyed being single, being free to travel, to come and go as I please," she says.

"Now I'm seriously looking for a husband. A widower would be fine. I think I'd make some lucky kid a great stepmother, don't you?"

• Carol, married and child-free, states, "When I do the things I do for my parents—when I phone them or fly down to Florida to see them; when I drive them to their doctors' appointments—I wonder to myself, *What's going to happen to me? Who is going to take care of me when I grow old?* And that dredges up a lot of feelings. It frightens me. What I *have* done is to make a pact with other friends who don't have children that, when the time comes that we need help, we will be there for each other."

And I? I have looked at studies of the differing involvement in parent care by sons and daughters, have read researcher Amy Horowitz's suggestion that "parents who can depend only upon sons are, to a certain extent, disadvantaged because they must do without the extra instrumental assistance that daughters provide," and this thought enters my mind: If women are the primary nurturers, what help can I expect from my three sons?

What We Can Do

Therapist and author Vivian Greenberg observes that more and more adult children in their sixties are going into therapy because they want to end well with their own children. She says, "We're determined not to repeat a pattern that our parents never knew ... because *their* parents died young." But our parents are living longer, and so we *do* know. And we are able to act on what we have learned and experienced.

For Verna, a long-distance caregiver, this has meant moving closer to her own grown children to make access possible if, in the future, she finds that she needs their help.

Arthur, a bachelor, has taken out a long-term health insurance policy, figuring that the cost is worth it for his peace of mind.

Phillipa and her husband recently put down a deposit on a condo in an adult community that is connected with a long-term-care facility. "If we ever get to the point where we find it difficult to manage a home or ourselves, we'll be taken care of," she says. "If you really want to have independence, you should choose (while you're able to choose) where to live, what your health care preferences are, and even leave funeral instructions, or else someone else will make those choices for you."

While we haven't gone that far, Noel and I have made out our health-care proxies, reviewed our insurance, brought our wills up to date—all things that we should have done under any circumstances but which became more immediately important because of our experience as caregivers. We also hold periodic discussions with our children. (Research studies notwithstanding, I'm not about to let my sons off the hook quite so easily.)

For those of us caregivers who have children, I think a cardinal rule of behavior has to be: *Do unto your children as you wish your parents had done unto you.* That often means sharing information with them: about our finances, insurance, health-care decisions, where we keep our tax records, where they will find the key to the safe-deposit box. These are not the most comfortable discussions, but they are necessary, for our sake and for theirs.

And I have told my sons: "If it someday becomes necessary for you to become involved in my care, I expect you to do what's right—for me and also for yourselves. I will not exact from you a promise that you will never put me in a nursing home . . . but if you do, I want to be sure it's the best possible home you can find."

"Oh, Mom, cut it out," they say, and immediately change the subject.

I cross my fingers, and life goes on.

Appendix A
Caregiver Bill of Rights*

ℭℬ

WE, THE CAREGIVERS, devote ourselves and our internal and external resources to the maintenance and support of a loved one.

We declare that we have basic inalienable rights:

The right to live our own life and retain our dignity and sense of self.

The right to choose a plan of caring that accommodates our needs and the needs of those we care about.

The right to be recognized as a vital and stabilizing source within our families.

The right to be free from any form of financial or legal coercion when choosing a plan for providing care.

The right to be free of guilt, anguish, and doubt, knowing that the decisions we make are appropriate for our own well-being and that of our loved one.

The right to be ourselves enough to have confidence that we are doing the best that we are able to do.

With these rights, the disabled and frail elderly will be provided with the highest and best care that we are capable of giving, and we may take pride in ourselves.

*Adapted from the Caregivers Network of the Natural Supports Program, 1981, Community Service Society of New York Model Project, Administration of Aging, #02AM48-02.

Appendix B
State Units on Aging

State Units on Aging offer information and referral services at no cost. The State Units on Aging can refer you to the local Area Agency on Aging, which will provide you with information on community resources.

ALABAMA
Martha Murph Beck
Executive Director
COMMISSION ON AGING
RSA Plaza, Suite 470
770 Washington Avenue
Montgomery, AL 36130
(205) 242-5743

ALASKA
Connie Sipe, Director
DIVISION OF SENIOR SERVICES
Department of Administration
3601 C St., #380
Anchorage, AK 99503
(907) 563-5654

ARIZONA
Richard Littler, Director
AGING AND ADULT
    ADMINISTRATION
Department of Economic Security
1789 W. Jefferson, #950A
Phoenix, AZ 85007
(602) 542-4446

ARKANSAS
Herb Sanderson, Director
DIVISION OF AGING & ADULT
    SERVICES
Arkansas Dept. of Human
    Services
P.O. Box 1437, Slot 1412

228

7th and Main Streets
Little Rock, AR 72201
(501) 682-2441

CALIFORNIA
Dixon Arnett, Director
DEPARTMENT OF AGING
1600 K Street
Sacramento, CA 95814
(916) 322-5290

COLORADO
Rita Barreras, Manager
DIVISION OF AGING AND
    ADULT SERVICES
Department of Social Services
110 16th St., 2nd fl.
Denver, CO 80203-1714
(303) 620-4147

CONNECTICUT
Christine Lewis, Director of
    Community Services
DEPARTMENT OF SOCIAL
    SERVICES ELDERLY SERVICES
    DIVISION
25 Sigourney St.
Hartford, CT 06106-5033
(203) 424-5281

DELAWARE
Eleanor Cain, Director
DIVISION OF SERVICES FOR
    AGING & ADULTS WITH
    PHYSICAL DISABILITIES

Department of Health & Social
    Services
1901 North DuPont Highway
New Castle, DE 19720
(302) 577-4791

DISTRICT OF COLUMBIA
Jearline Williams, Executive
    Director
OFFICE ON AGING
One Judiciary Square
441 4th St., NW, 9th fl.
Washington, DC 20001
(202) 724-5622

FLORIDA
Bentley Lipscomb, Secretary
DEPARTMENT OF ELDER
    AFFAIRS
Building B, Room 152
4040 Esplanade Way
Tallahassee, FL 32399-0700
(904) 414-2000

GEORGIA
Judy Hagebak, Director
OFFICE OF AGING
#2 Peachtree St. N.E., 18th fl.
Atlanta, GA 30303
(404) 657-5258

GUAM
Florence P. Shimizu
Administrator
DIVISION OF SENIOR
    CITIZENS

Department of Public Health &
 Social Services
Government of Guam
P.O. Box 2816
Agana, Guam 96910
011 (671) 734-4361

HAWAII
Marilyn Seely, Director
EXECUTIVE OFFICE ON
 AGING
Office of the Governor
335 Merchant St., Room 241
Honolulu, HI 96813
(808) 586-0100

IDAHO
Jesse Berain, Director
OFFICE ON AGING
Room 108, Statehouse
Boise, ID 83720
(208) 334-3833

ILLINOIS
Maralee Lindley, Director
DEPARTMENT ON AGING
421 East Capitol Avenue
Springfield, IL 62701
(217) 785-2870

INDIANA
Geneva Shedd, Director
BUREAU OF AGING/IN-HOME
 SERVICES
402 W. Washington St., #E-431

Indianapolis, IN 46207-7083
(317) 232-7020

IOWA
Betty Grandquist, Executive
 Director
DEPARTMENT OF ELDER
 AFFAIRS
Jewett Bldg., Suite 236
914 Grand Avenue
Des Moines, IA 50309
(515) 281-5187

KANSAS
Thelma Hunter Gordon, Director
DEPARTMENT ON AGING
Docking State Office Bldg., 122-S
915 S.W. Harrison
Topeka, KS 66612-1500
(913) 296-4986

KENTUCKY
S. Jack Williams, Director
DIVISION OF AGING
 SERVICES
Cabinet for Human Resources
275 East Main Street, 6 West
Frankfort, KY 40621
(502) 564-6930

LOUISIANA
Robert Fontenot, Director
OFFICE OF ELDERLY AFFAIRS
P.O. Box 80374
4550 N. Blvd., 2nd fl.

Baton Rouge, LA 70806
(504) 925-1700

MAINE
Christine Gianopoulos, Director
BUREAU OF ELDER & ADULT
   SERVICES
Department of Human Services
State House, Station #11
Augusta, ME 04333
(207) 624-5335

MARIANA ISLANDS
John C. Leon Guerrero, Director
Division of Veterans Affairs—
   DC&CA
Office of the Governors
Commonwealth of the Northern
   Mariana Islands
Saipan, MP 96950
(670) 234-6011/6696

MARYLAND
Sue Ward, Director
OFFICE ON AGING
State Office Building, Room
   1004
301 West Preston Street
Baltimore, MD 21201
(410) 225-1100

MASSACHUSETTS
Franklin Ollivierre, Secretary
EXECUTIVE OFFICE OF ELDER
   AFFAIRS

1 Ashburton Place, 5th fl.
Boston, MA 02108
(617) 727-7750

MICHIGAN
Diane Braunstein, Director
OFFICE OF SERVICES TO THE
   AGING
P.O. Box 80026
Lansing, MI 48909
(517) 373-8230

MINNESOTA
Jim Varpness
Executive Director
BOARD ON AGING
444 Lafayette Road
St. Paul, MN 55155-3843
(612) 296-2770

MISSISSIPPI
Eddie Anderson, Director
COUNCIL ON AGING
Division of Aging & Adult
   Services
750 N. State St.
Jackson, MS 39202
(601) 359-4929

MISSOURI
Gregg Vadner, Director
DIVISION ON AGING
Department of Social Services
P.O. Box 1337
615 Howerton Court

Jefferson City, MO 65102-1337
(314) 751-3082

MONTANA
Charles Rehbein
Acting Aging Coordinator
GOVERNOR'S OFFICE ON
   AGING
State Capitol Bldg.
Capitol Station, Room 219
Helena, MT 59620
(406) 444-3111

NEBRASKA
Dennis Loose, Director
DEPARTMENT ON AGING
P.O. Box 95044
301 Centennial Mall-South
Lincoln, NE 68509
(402) 471-2306

NEVADA
Suzanne Ernst, Administrator
DIVISION FOR AGING
   SERVICES
Department of Human Resources
State Mail Room Complex
Las Vegas, NV 89158
(702) 486-3545

NEW HAMPSHIRE
Ronald Adcock, Director
DIVISION OF ELDERLY &
   ADULT SERVICES
State Office Park South

115 Pleasant St. Annex Bldg. #1
Concord, NH 03301-3843
(603) 271-4680

NEW JERSEY
Ruth Reader, Director
DIVISION ON AGING
Department of Community Affairs
CN 807
South Broad and Front Streets
Trenton, NJ 08625-0807
(609) 984-6693

NEW MEXICO
Michelle Lujan-Grisham, Director
STATE AGENCY ON AGING
La Villa Rivera Bldg.
224 East Palace Avenue, 4th fl.
Santa Fe, NM 87501
(505) 827-7640

NEW YORK
Walter Hoefer, Director
OFFICE FOR THE AGING
New York State Plaza
Agency Building #2
Albany, NY 12223
(518) 474-4425

NORTH CAROLINA
Bonnie Cramer, Director
DIVISION OF AGING
CB 29531
693 Palmer Drive
Raleigh, NC 27626-0531
(919) 733-3983

NORTH DAKOTA
Linda Wright, Director
AGING SERVICES DIVISION
Department of Human Services
P.O. Box 7070, Northbrook Shop
  Ctr.
North Washington Street
Bismarck, ND 58507-7070
(701) 328-2577

OHIO
Judith Brachman, Director
DEPARTMENT OF AGING
50 West Broad Street, 9th fl.
Columbus, OH 43266-0501
(614) 466-5500

OKLAHOMA
Roy Keen, Division
  Administrator
AGING SERVICES
  DIVISION
Department of Human
  Services
P.O. Box 25352
312 N.E. 28th Street
Oklahoma City, OK 73125
(405) 521-2327

OREGON
Jim Wilson, Administrator
SENIOR & DISABLED SERVICES
  DIVISION
500 Summer St., NE, 2nd fl.

Salem, OR 97310-1015
(503) 945-5811

REPUBLIC OF PALAU
Lillian Nakamura, Director
AGENCY ON AGING
P.O. Box 100
Koror, PW 96940

PENNSYLVANIA
Richard Browdie, Secretary
DEPARTMENT OF AGING
MSS Office Building
400 Market St., 7th fl.
Harrisburg, PA 17101-2301
(717) 783-1550

PUERTO RICO
Ruby Rodriguez, Executive
  Director
GOVERNOR'S OFFICE FOR
  ELDERLY AFFAIRS
Corbian Plaza, Stop 23
Ponce De Leon Avenue #1603
U.M. Office C
San Ture, PR 00908
(809) 721-5710

RHODE ISLAND
Barbara Ruffino, Director
DEPARTMENT OF ELDERLY
  AFFAIRS
160 Pine Street
Providence, RI 02903-3708
(401) 277-2858

(AMERICAN) SAMOA
Tauala Luavasa, Director
TERRITORIAL ADMINISTRATION
ON AGING
American Samoa Government
Pago Pago, American Samoa
96799
011 (684) 633-1252

SOUTH CAROLINA
Constance Rinehart, Director
DIVISION ON AGING
Office of the Governor
202 Arbor Lake Dr., #301
Columbia, SC 29223
(803) 737-7500

SOUTH DAKOTA
Gail Ferris, Executive Director
OFFICE OF ADULT SERVICES &
AGING
700 Governors Drive
Pierre, SD 57501
(605) 773-3656

TENNESSEE
Emily Wiseman, Executive
Director
COMMISSION ON
AGING
Andrew Jackson Bldg.
500 Deaderick Bldg., 9th fl.
Nashville, TN 37243-0860
(615) 741-2056

TEXAS
Mary Sapp, Executive Director
DEPARTMENT ON AGING
P.O. Box 12786 Capitol
Station
1949 IH 35, South
Austin, TX 78741-3702
(512) 444-2727

UTAH
Helen Goddard, Director
DIVISION OF AGING & ADULT
SERVICES
Department of Social Services
Box 45500
120 North, 200 West
Salt Lake City, UT 84145-0500
(801) 538-3910

VERMONT
Lawrence Crist, Commissioner
AGING AND DISABILITIES
103 South Main Street
Waterbury, VT 05676
(802) 241-2400

VIRGINIA
Thelma Bland, Commissioner
DEPARTMENT FOR THE
AGING
700 Centre, 10th fl.
700 East Franklin Street
Richmond, VA 23219-2327
(804) 225-2271

VIRGIN ISLANDS
Bernice Hall, Administrator
SENIOR CITIZENS AFFAIRS
Department of Human Services
#19 Estate Diamond
  Fredericksted
St. Croix, VI 00840
(809) 772-4950, ext. 46

WASHINGTON
Charles Reed, Assistant Secretary
AGING & ADULT SERVICES
  ADMINISTRATION
Department of Social & Health
  Services
P.O. Box 45050
Olympia, WA 98504-5050
(206) 586-3768

WEST VIRGINIA
David Brown, Interim Executive
  Director

OFFICE OF AGING
Department of Health and
  Human Resources
Holly Grove, State Capitol
Charleston, WV 25305
(304) 558-3317

WISCONSIN
Donna McDowell, Director
BUREAU OF AGING
Division of Community
  Services
217 S. Hamilton St., Suite 300
Madison, WI 53707
(608) 266-2536

WYOMING
Morris Gardner, Administrator
COMMISSION ON AGING
Hathaway Building, Room 139
Cheyenne, WY 82002-0710
(307) 777-7986

Appendix C
Helpful Organizations and Resources

Eldercare Locator
National toll-free number: (800) 677-1116
A nationwide service administered by The National Association of Area Agencies on Aging to help families find information about a wide range of community services for older people: services such as home-delivered meals; transportation; legal assistance; housing options; recreation and social activities; adult day care; senior center programs; home health services; elder abuse prevention; nursing home ombudsmen.

Call between 9:00 A.M. and 11:00 P.M. Have the following information ready: the name and address of the older person—most important, the zip code to aid in identifying the nearest information and assistance sources; a brief general description of the problem or type of assistance you are seeking.

American Association of Retired Persons (AARP)
601 E Street, NW
Washington, DC 20049
(202) 434-2560
In addition to its advocacy agenda, AARP publishes helpful brochures and pamphlets, including a free *Caregiver Resource Kit,* including "Miles Away and Still Caring," a booklet for long-distance caregivers. To receive a copy, write to AARP Fulfillment (EE0756), P.O. Box 22796, Long Beach, CA 90801-5796.

Children of Aging Parents (CAPS)
Woodbourne Office Campus
Suite 302A
1609 Woodbourne Road
Levittown, PA 19057
(215) 945-6900
Individual caregiver dues are $20 per year. Covers subscription to a newsletter and resources and information on a national level, including referral to existing caregiver support groups nationwide.

Friends and Relatives of Institutionalized Aged (FRIA)
11 John Street, Suite 601
New York, NY 10038
(212) 732-4455
New York-based FRIA provides information about long-term-care options and helps families learn to become effective advocates. Ask about publications, including the pamphlet "Comprehensive Care Planning."

National Academy of Elder Law Attorneys
1604 North Country Club Road
Tucson, AZ 85716
(602) 881-4005
Provides information and referrals to attorneys specializing in elder law.

National Association for Home Care
519 C Street, NE
Washington, DC 20002
(202) 547-7424
Request a copy of a brochure titled "How to Choose a Home Care Agency."

National Association of Professional Geriatric Care Managers
1604 North Country Club Road
Tucson, AZ 85716
(602) 881-8008
Provides referrals to professional geriatric care managers nationwide.

National Citizens Coalition for Nursing Home Reform
1424 16th Street, NW
Suite 202
Washington, DC 20036
(202) 332-2275
Call for information on ombudsman or consumer groups in your area
or for help in solving a specific problem regarding nursing home care.

National Council on Aging (NCOA)
409 Third Street, SW
2nd fl.
Washington, DC 20024
(202) 479-1200
The NCOA is a comprehensive membership association for professionals, organizations, volunteers, and individuals who provide care
and services to older persons and their families. It has eleven "con-
stituent units," including those specializing in Financial Issues and
Services for Elders, National Institute on Adult Daycare, etc. This
organization is geared toward people who work in gerontology-
related fields; individual members may find the publications, including
their *Perspectives on Aging* magazine, helpful. *Note: The National Institute on Adult Daycare can also be reached at this address and phone
number.*

National Family Caregivers Association
9621 East Bexhill Drive
Kensington, MD 20895-3104
(301) 942-6430
Dedicated to improving the life of family caregivers through educational outreach, research, support, and validation. Publishes a quarterly newsletter, *Take Care!*, and maintains a support network linking
caregivers. Individual caregiver dues are $10 per year.

National Institute on Aging
9000 Rockville Pike
Bethesda, MD 20892
(301) 496-1752 or (800) 222-2225
Conducts and supports research, training, information dissemination,
and programs related to aging.

238

National Self-Help Clearinghouse
(212) 354-8525
Provides information and referral to support groups nationwide.

SPECIALIZED RESOURCES

Alzheimer's Association
919 North Michigan Avenue
Chicago, IL 60611-1676
(312) 335-8700 or (800) 272-3900
Provides information on the illness and referrals to medical resources, as well as to local chapters, publications, and support.

American Cancer Society
(800) 227-2345
Links callers to local chapters, where they can receive information on programs, publications, and support groups.

American Diabetes Association
1660 Duke Street
Alexandria, VA 22314
(800) DIABETES
Provides information on the illness, referrals to doctors and registered dieticians, lists of local chapters and support groups, and publications. Membership includes subscription to monthly magazine, *Forecasts*, plus announcements of local programs.

American Heart Association
7272 Greenville Avenue
Dallas, TX 75231
(800) 242-8721
Callers are connected to the local affiliate, which provides educational material regarding heart disease and stroke, plus information on support groups for patients and caregivers.

Arthritis Foundation Information Line
(800) 283-7800
Free brochures, doctor referral list, support groups, and self-help groups. Ask about their publication, *Arthritis Today*.

Cancer Care
1180 Avenue of the Americas
New York, NY 10036
(212) 221-3300
The largest agency in the country solely dedicated to providing emotional and financial support to cancer patients and their families, plus community education, at no cost. Has offices in New York, New Jersey, and Connecticut, plus a toll-free counseling line, (800) 813-HOPE, in Florida and Delaware.

Help for Incontinent People (HIP)
P.O. Box 544
Union, SC 29379
(800) BLADDER
Publishes *The HIP Report*, a quarterly newsletter that provides moral support and practical information, as well as a Resource Guide listing products and services that can help.

Lighthouse National Center for Vision and Aging
111 East 59th Street
New York, NY 10022
(800) 334-5497
Provides information and referrals to agencies that help older adults and their families with problems of vision and aging. Publications catalog available.

National Institute of Neurological Disorders and Stroke
P.O. Box 5801
Bethesda, MD 20824
(800) 352-9424
Provides public and professionals with information, educational materials, and research highlights. Refers patients and caregivers to support groups.

240

National Parkinson's Foundation
1501 NW Ninth Avenue
Miami, FL 33136
(800) 327-4545; in Florida, (800) 433-7022; in California,
(800) 400-8448
Provides educational materials, referrals to medical centers and
specialists throughout the country, and information about support
groups.

National Stroke Association
8480 East Orchard Road
Suite 1000
Englewood, CO 80111-5015
(800) 787-6537
Provides informational pamphlets, booklets, and referrals to chapters
and support groups. Publishes *The Road Ahead,* a book that caregivers
will find helpful. Staff members are available to answer questions.

APPENDIX D
Suggested Reading

Cohen, Donna, and Carl Eisdorfer, *Seven Steps to Effective Parent Care*. New York: Tarcher/Putnam, 1993. Gerontologists Cohen and Eisdorfer lay out a process of problem solving that can help caregivers address the issues, avoid family battles, and generally feel more able. A thoughtful book.

Edinberg, Mark A. *Talking with Your Aging Parents*. Boston, Mass.: Shambhala, 1987. The author counsels readers on how to talk with aging relatives about difficult issues like failing health, legal and financial matters, and family relations.

Greenberg, Vivian. *Children of a Certain Age: Adults and Their Aging Parents*. New York: Macmillan, 1994. The author stresses the interdependence of family members, offering guidance on ways parents and children can learn to accept one another, warts and all.

Greenberg, Vivian. *Your Best Is Good Enough: Aging Parents and Your Emotions*. New York: Lexington Books, 1989.

Halpern, James. *Helping Your Aging Parents: A Practical Guide for Adult Children*. New York: Fawcett Crest, 1987. A family therapist, Halpern addresses the issues from a family systems perspective. A helpful approach.

Heath, Angela. *Long Distance Caregiving*. Lakewood, Colo.: American Source Books, 1993. A practical guide that gives step-by-step instructions on how to organize and monitor care from far away.

Rob, Caroline, with Janet Reynolds. *The Caregiver's Guide*. Boston, Mass.: Houghton Mifflin, l991. Strong on practical advice: here's what's wrong, here's how to respond.

242

Siegal, Alan P., and Robert S. Siegal, *Forget Me Not: Caring and Coping with Your Aging Parents*. Berkeley, Calif.: Celestial Arts, 1993. This book guides caregivers along a difficult journey that involves making many decisions. It is especially strong in providing medical explanations and helping families deal with the medical profession.

Silverstone, Barbara, and Helen Kandel Hyman. *You and Your Aging Parent*, 3rd ed. New York: Pantheon, 1989. Practical advice for caregivers, from a general overview of the aging process to advice on managing specific issues: medical, psychological, and financial.

Werner, Anne P., and James P. Firman. *Home Care for Older People: A Consumer's Guide*, revised edition. Washington, DC: United Seniors Health Cooperative, 1993. Covers such issues as choosing a home-care provider; managing care; measuring the quality of care; involving family and friends; paying for home care. A practical guide.

BOOKS ON ALZHEIMER'S DISEASE

Aronson, Miriam K. *Understanding Alzheimer's Disease*. New York: Charles Scribner's Sons, 1988.

Mace, Nancy L., and Peter V. Rabins. *The 36-Hour Day*. New York: Warner Books, 1992. The classic book on caring for persons with Alzheimer's disease.

BIBLIOGRAPHY

Anderson, Ellis, and Marsha Dryan. *Aging Parents & You*. New York
    Master Media Limited, 1988.

Blyskal, Jeff. "Caring for Aging Parents," *McCall's*, September 1993.

Brooks, Andrée. "Helping the Elderly at Home," *New York Times*, February 9, 1995.

Butler, Robert. *Why Survive? Being Old in America*. New York: Harper
    & Row, 1975.

Cadmus, Robert R. *Caring for Your Aging Parents*. Englewood Cliffs,
    N.J.: Prentice-Hall, 1984.

Cohen, Donna, and Carl Eisdorfer. *Seven Steps to Effective Parent Care*.
    New York: Tarcher/Putnam, 1993.

Cole, Al. "From a Distance," *Modern Maturity*, March–April 1995.

Doress, Paula Brown, Diana Laskin Siegel, and The Midlife and
    Older Women Book Project, *Ourselves, Growing Older*. New York:
    Touchstone/Simon & Schuster, 1987.

Farran, Carol J., and Eleanora Keane-Hagerty. "Twelve Steps for Caregivers," *The American Journal of Alzheimer's Care and Related
    Disorders Research,* November–December 1989.

Fein, Esther B. "Caring at Home and Burning Out," *New York Times,*
    December 19, 1994.

Greenberg, Vivian E. *Your Best Is Good Enough: Aging Parents and
    Your Emotions*. New York: Lexington Books, 1989.

———. *Children of a Certain Age: Adults and Their Aging Parents*.
    New York: Macmillan, 1994.

Greer, Rebecca E. "A Nursing Home? For *My* Mom?" *Woman's Day*, July
    21, 1992.

Halpern, James. *Helping Your Aging Parents: A Practical Guide for
    Adult Children*. New York: Fawcett Crest, 1987.

Heath, Angela. *Long Distance Caregiving*. Lakewood, Colo.: American
    Source Books, 1993.

244

Horowitz, Amy. "Family Caregiving to the Frail Elderly," *Annual Review of Gerontology and Geriatrics,* edited by M. P. Lawton and G. Maddox. New York: Springer Publishing, 1985.

———. "Methodological Issues in the Study of Gender Within Family Caregiving Relationships," *Gender, Families, and Elder Care,* ed. Jeffrey W. Dwyer and Raymond T. Coward. Newbury Park, Calif.: Sage Publications, 1991.

———. "Sons and Daughters as Caregivers to Older Parents: Differences in Role Performance and Consequences," *The Gerontologist* 25, no. 6, 1985.

Horowitz, Amy, and Rose Dobrof, co-principal investigators, The Brookdale Center on Aging of Hunter College. "The Role of Families in Providing Long-Term Care to the Frail and Chronically Ill Elderly Living in the Community." Final Report submitted to the Health Care Financing Administration, Department of Health and Human Services, May 1982.

Horowitz, Amy, and Lois W. Shindelman. "Reciprocity and Affection: Past Influences on Current Caregiving," *Journal of Gerontological Social Work* 5, no. 3 (Spring 1983).

Horowitz, Amy, Barbara M. Silverstone, and Joann P. Reinhardt. "A Conceptual and Empirical Exploration of Personal Autonomy Issues Within Family Caregiving Relationships," *The Gerontologist* 31, no. 1 (1991).

Jarvik, Lissy, and Gary Small. *Parentcare: A Commonsense Guide for Adult Children,* New York: Crown Publishers, 1988.

Kübler-Ross, Elisabeth. *On Death and Dying.* New York: Macmillan, 1970.

Mace, Nancy L, and Peter V. Rabins. *The 36-Hour Day.* New York: Warner Books, 1992.

McLeod, Beth Witrogen, and Annie Nakao. "The Caregivers," *San Francisco Examiner,* April 2–7, 1995.

Nuland, Sherwin B. *How We Die.* New York: Alfred A. Knopf, 1994.

Pritikin, Enid, and Trudy Reece. *Parentcare Survival Guide.* Hauppauge, New York: Barron's, 1993.

Rob, Caroline, with Janet Reynolds. *The Caregiver's Guide.* Boston, Mass.: Houghton Mifflin, 1991.

Roth, Philip. *Patrimony.* New York: Simon & Schuster, 1991.

Siegal, Alan P., and Robert S. Siegal. *Forget Me Not.* Berkeley, Calif: Celestial Arts, 1993.

Silverstone, Barbara, and Helen Kandel Hyman. *You and Your Aging Parent,* third edition. New York: Pantheon, 1989.

Silverstone, Barbara, and Amy Horowitz. "Aging in Place: The Role of Families," *Generations,* Spring 1992.

Suitor, J. Jill, and Karl Pillemer. "Family Caregiving and Marital Satisfaction: Findings From a One-Year Panel Study of Women Caring for Parents With Dementia," *Journal of Marriage and the Family,* August 1994.

————. "Support and Interpersonal Stress in the Social Networks of Married Daughters Caring for Parents With Dementia," *Journal of Gerontology* 1 (1993).

Weinstein, Grace W. *The Lifetime Book of Money Management,* third edition. Detroit, Mich.: Visible Ink Press, 1993.

————. "Helping Your Parents Cope," *Kiplinger's Personal Finance Magazine,* March 1994.

INDEX